# KOREAN COOKING
## FAVORITES

# KOREAN COOKING
## FAVORITES

### KIMCHI, BBQ, BIBIMBAP
### AND SO MUCH MORE

## HYEGYOUNG K. FORD
### FOUNDER OF BEYOND KIMCHEE

PAGE STREET
PUBLISHING CO.

PAGE STREET
PUBLISHING CO.

First published in 2019 by

Page Street Publishing Co.

27 Congress Street, Suite 105

Salem, MA  01970

www.pagestreetpublishing.com

Distributed by Macmillan, sales in Canada by The Canadian Manda Group.

23   22   21   20   19     1   2   3   4   5

ISBN-13: 978-1-62414-869-9

ISBN-10: 1-62414-869-7

Library of Congress Control Number:  2019932079

Cover and book design by Laura Gallant for Page Street Publishing Co.

Photography by Hyegyoung K. Ford

Printed and bound in China

TO MY MOTHER, THE STRONGEST YET THE MOST
LOVING WOMAN I KNOW.

AND TO MY HUSBAND, BEN, AND MY TWO
CHILDREN, LAUREN AND PRESTON.

THIS BOOK IS FOR YOU.

# CONTENTS

# INTRODUCTION

You can take the girl out of Korea, but you cannot take Korea out of the girl.

I was born and raised in a fishing town called Tongyoung, located at the southern tip of South Korea. My hometown is famous in Korea as one of our most beautiful places to live. The city is surrounded by water dotted with "floating" islands, like green mounds that emerge from the sea. That striking sea vista and the tranquil inland hills and fields gave me a great appreciation of the beauty and abundance of nature.

Since my youth, I have spent more than half of my life outside of Korea, living and traveling in various countries in both hemispheres. I learned to appreciate the diversity of different cultures and their food, which inspired me to become a foodie. At the end of the day, however, when I need my comfort, I always look to Korean food, the food of my childhood.

I grew up eating every meal made from scratch with locally grown ingredients. Thanks to my mother who devotedly rose at five o'clock each morning and walked to the local market to buy the fresh meat, fish and vegetables she needed for the day, I never knew what processed or packaged food was. My mother believed that food made with fresh ingredients and love helps build a healthy mind and body. Her food was generally not fancy or complicated; rather, it was simple and homey. She never used recipes and never measured or weighed anything. "A little bit of this or that" is the only way she can describe her cooking. Like most Korean mothers of her generation, she never owned a cookbook. She learned most of her cooking looking over the shoulder of her own mother, who was a famous cook in her hometown. Our family cooking legacy continues now, as I record these precious recipes in print and digitally.

I started my Korean food blog, Beyond Kimchee (www.beyondkimchee.com), in 2010. At first, it was simply for my children. I wanted to keep a record of all the recipes that I, and they, grew up eating. My blog was a gift to them, so that they will continue to appreciate their Korean heritage through food when I am no longer with them. Since I started the blog publicly, I have received numerous heartfelt personal messages from my readers, Koreans and non-Koreans both, from all over the world. These are not lab-tested, scientifically derived formulas. The love and sincerity in these recipes cannot be denied, and it has connected many people of different backgrounds.

I am neither a trained chef nor do I work in the food industry. In this cookbook, however, you will find generations of training and wisdom behind some of the most valuable, authentic homestyle Korean dishes. To the childhood recipes I learned from my mother and my aunts, I have added my own personality and insight. Success in Korean cooking depends not only on the recipe itself, but even more on the know-how and cooking technique. That is why I have included many cooking and other kitchen tips on how to succeed with these scrumptious Korean dishes, even in a Western kitchen. Life is much more complicated and fast-paced now than decades ago. I don't get up at five o'clock in the morning to walk to the local market as my mother did. However, I do prepare my Korean meals with the freshest ingredients possible, and I make them easy to prepare so that anyone who follows my recipes and tips can enjoy the same delicious and healthy Korean fare.

Korean food is the cuisine of love and devotion. Some Korean dishes even teach you to be patient. The lesson of good food is to take a break from our busy moments, genuinely interact with and care for one another and love life itself.

So, cook up some delicious Korean food and share it with your loved ones. The recipes in this book will make you feel as though you are in a loving Korean home.

# SAVORY
# SNACKS

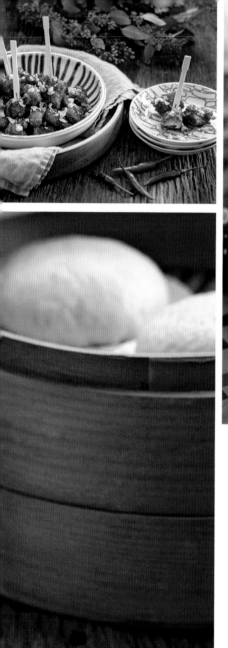

**KOREA** offers a cornucopia of snacks and finger foods. You can find them everywhere: city street vendors, rural markets and even in fancy restaurants. From chewy rice cakes to paradigm-shifting Korean fried chicken to crispy savory pancakes—all are easily found in Korea . . . and did you know they can also be made easily at home?

Some are spicy, some sweet and some, of course, are salty. Korean snacks will launch your taste buds to another level.

These snacks can be an appetizer, party food or even a quick, simple meal. Try throwing a Korean snack party with family and friends to enjoy them all! (No plane ticket to Korea necessary.)

# SPICY KOREAN FRIED CHICKEN

**(MAEUN YANGNYUM CHICKEN, 매운양념치킨)**

## SERVES 4

KFC anyone? Korean fried chicken is now world-famous, even though those three letters are generally associated with another type of fried chicken. But who wouldn't love the sticky, finger-licking deliciousness of crisp chicken wings slathered with a spicy sauce? Yes, these wings are spicy, but they are worth every bead of sweat they might inspire. Korean-style fried chicken is often served with a cold beverage, such as beer or a carbonated drink. In fact, it is often referred to as chimak, which is a combination of the English word chicken and the Korean word for beer (maekju). Go on an adventure next Friday evening after work with these hot chicken wings and a cold drink to recover from your hectic week, just as the Koreans do.

### CHICKEN

3 lb (1.4 kg) chicken party wings

1 tsp salt

1 tsp pureed fresh ginger

½ tsp freshly ground black pepper

1 tbsp (15 ml) sweet rice wine (mirin)

Peanut oil, for deep-frying

1 cup (128 g) cornstarch

¼ cup (30 g) finely chopped walnuts, for garnish

### SWEET CHILI SAUCE

½ small onion

2 cloves garlic, finely minced

2 tbsp (33 g) Korean chili paste

1 tbsp (6 g) Korean chili flakes

2 tbsp (30 ml) soy sauce

2 tbsp (30 g) ketchup

2 tbsp (30 ml) sweet rice wine (mirin)

3 tbsp (39 g) sugar

2 tbsp (40 g) apricot preserves

2 tbsp (30 ml) water

In a large bowl, toss the chicken wings with the salt, ginger, black pepper and rice wine; set them aside for 15 minutes.

Prepare the sauce. Grate the onion on a fine cheese grater and place it in a small pot. Add the rest of the sauce ingredients and mix well. Place the pot over medium-high heat and bring to a gentle boil. Lower the heat to low and simmer for 3 to 4 minutes; remove it from the heat and set it aside.

In a large pot, heat the oil over medium heat until it reaches 350°F (175°C).

Put the cornstarch into a large, resealable plastic bag. Add the chicken wings to the bag and shake well to coat them evenly. Remove the wings from the bag, shaking off the excess starch. Working a small batch at a time, deep-fry the wings until they're pale golden brown, 3 to 4 minutes. Using a metal strainer, remove the chicken from the oil and give each piece a little shake to remove any excess oil. Transfer the chicken to a paper towel–lined plate and let them sit for 5 minutes.

Return the first batch of chicken to the pot for the second deep-frying and cook until the wings turn slightly dark golden brown, 2 to 3 minutes. Finish the rest of chicken wings in the same method.

Using a pastry brush, brush the wings with the sauce and sprinkle the chopped walnuts on top. Serve hot or at room temperature.

**COOK'S TIP:** If you want to try a more exotic flavor, try adding 2 teaspoons (4 g) of curry powder to the chicken when you marinate the wings. It adds another layer of piquancy and goes really well with the chili paste.

## (GANJANG YANGNYUM CHICKEN, 간장양념치킨)

SOY-GLAZED KOREAN
FRIED CHICKEN

# SOY-GLAZED KOREAN FRIED CHICKEN

## SERVES 4

### SOY GLAZE

¼ cup (60 ml) soy sauce

1 tbsp (15 ml) oyster sauce

3 tbsp (39 g) sugar

½ cup (120 ml) water

6 to 8 cloves garlic, thinly sliced

½ medium onion, chopped

1 tbsp (8 g) cornstarch

2 tbsp (30 g) grated Korean radish or daikon radish

1 (3" [7.5-cm]) piece dried sea kelp

2 or 3 thin lemon slices

### CHICKEN

3 lb (1.4 kg) chicken party wings and drumettes

2 tbsp (30 ml) sweet rice wine (mirin)

1 tsp pureed fresh ginger

½ tsp salt

¼ tsp freshly ground black pepper

½ cup (64 g) cornstarch

2 tbsp (15 g) all-purpose flour

¼ tsp baking powder

Peanut oil or other oil suitable for deep-frying

Roasted sesame seeds, for garnish (optional)

Just because a dish is Korean does not always mean that it is spicy. Take, for example, this amazing Korean fried chicken. These succulent chicken wings boast a delightfully crisp texture and are coated with a gently sweetened soy sauce glaze that carries a burst of flavor. Do not skip the radish and the dried sea kelp in the sauce—they are the secret ingredients that really make these wings stand out from ordinary wings. This recipe is as close as you can get to any franchised Korean fried chicken, if not better.

In a small pot, prepare the glaze. Combine all the glaze ingredients, except the lemon, and bring it to a gentle boil over medium-high heat. Lower the heat to low, remove the sea kelp and add the lemon slices. Simmer, uncovered, for 5 to 7 minutes. Strain the sauce over a bowl, pressing down with a wooden spoon, to collect the syrup. Discard the parts that did not pass through the strainer. Set the syrup aside to cool to room temperature. The glaze will continue to thicken as it cools.

Marinate the chicken. In a large bowl, toss the chicken wings and drumettes with the rice wine, ginger, salt and pepper. Let them sit for 15 minutes.

In a large, resealable plastic bag, combine the cornstarch, flour and baking powder. Drop the marinated chicken into the bag and shake well to coat them evenly.

To deep-fry, in a large pot, heat the oil to 350°F (175°C) over medium-high heat. Remove the chicken pieces from the bag and shake off the excess starch. Working in small batches, deep-fry the chicken until they're pale golden brown, 3 to 4 minutes. Remove them from the oil and transfer them to a paper towel–lined plate.

When all the chicken pieces are fried, deep-fry them a second time until they are deep golden brown and crispy, 2 to 3 minutes, adjusting the heat to avoid browning them too quickly.

Using a pastry brush, brush the chicken with the glaze. Garnish with sesame seeds, if using, and serve warm.

**COOK'S TIP:** The glaze can be stored in the refrigerator for up to 2 weeks. If you want to make the chicken ahead of time, you can do the first deep-frying up to 2 hours in advance. When you are ready to serve, you can do the second frying and brush the chicken with the glaze. Expect a lot of oohs and aahs from your guests.

## CRISPY KOREAN CHICKEN NUGGETS

**(DAKGANGJEONG, 닭강정)**

**SERVES 4**

### CHICKEN

1 lb (455 g) boneless, skinless chicken thighs or breast, cut into bite-size pieces

1 tbsp (15 ml) sweet rice wine (mirin)

½ tsp salt

¼ tsp freshly ground black pepper

1 tsp pureed fresh ginger

2 tsp (10 ml) sesame oil

3 tbsp (24 g) cornstarch

3 tbsp (24 g) potato starch

Peanut oil or other oil suitable for deep-frying

1 or 2 red and/or green chile, thinly sliced

3 tbsp (27 g) peanuts, chopped, for garnish

### STICKY GLAZE

1 tbsp (15 ml) cooking oil

1 tbsp (15 ml) soy sauce

5 tbsp (75 ml) rice syrup or corn syrup

2 tbsp (26 g) sugar

1 tbsp (15 ml) cider vinegar or rice vinegar

These crispy little chicken nuggets are often confused with Korean fried chicken. Whereas Korean fried chicken is coated with a thin, glazelike gochujang-based sauce after the chicken is deep-fried, dakgangjeong is cooked in a much thicker and stickier, almost taffylike glaze. Good dakgangjeong will retain its crisp yet sticky texture long after it cools. Authentic dakgangjeong sauce is made with pure taffy that comes from barley sugar. Since it is hard to find outside Korea, you can mimic the texture with rice syrup (jochung) or corn syrup. Although the authentic version of dakgangjeong used to be made with boned chicken cut into small chunks, boneless is so much easier to eat and tastes equally good.

In a large bowl, combine the chicken with the rice wine, salt, black pepper, ginger and sesame oil; toss well and let it sit for 15 minutes.

Put the starches into a large, resealable plastic bag and add the chicken pieces. Shake the bag so the starches will coat the chicken evenly.

Heat the oil to 350°F (175°C). Working in small batches, deep-fry the chicken until they're light golden brown, 2 to 3 minutes. Using a metal strainer, remove the chicken from the oil. Shake the chicken pieces well to remove any excess oil. Transfer them to a wire rack or a paper towel–lined plate and let them rest for a few minutes. Then, deep-fry the chicken pieces again for a second time to a deep golden brown, 1 to 2 minutes, to ensure their crispiness. Transfer the chicken to a wire rack.

For the glaze, in a large skillet, combine the oil, soy sauce, syrup, sugar and vinegar and bring it to a boil over medium-high heat, stirring frequently. Reduce the sauce until it becomes a thick glaze, 1 to 2 minutes.

Lower the heat to low. Add the chicken along with the chile to the sauce and mix well. Let it simmer for another minute. Transfer the chicken to a serving platter and garnish with the chopped peanuts. The sauce will harden as it cools, making the chicken crispier yet still sticky. Serve warm or at room temperature.

## (SHIGUMCHI SAEWOO JEON, 시금치새우전)

1 cup (125 g) all-purpose flour

2 tbsp (16 g) cornstarch

¾ cup (180 ml) + 1 to 2 tbsp (15 to 30 ml) ice water, as needed

3 oz (85 g) baby spinach

½ medium onion, thinly sliced

8 oz (225 g) shrimp, shelled, cleaned and diced

4 tbsp (60 ml) oil, plus more as needed, divided

### DIPPING SAUCE

2 tbsp (30 ml) soy sauce

1 tbsp (15 ml) fresh lemon juice or rice vinegar

1½ tsp (3 g) Korean chili flakes (optional)

# SPINACH-SHRIMP PANCAKES
## MAKES 4 INDIVIDUAL-SIZE PANCAKES

These savory pancakes are super easy and quick. The golden, crispy pancake crust surrounds the soft, mellow spinach and the tender shrimp. Together, they create a scrumptious contrast with the tangy dipping sauce. You will forget that you are eating spinach, which makes it perfect for those who don't appreciate the greens. You never know—these pancakes might convert them! You can replace the shrimp with squid or mussels, or use a mixture of all of them.

In a large bowl, combine the flour, cornstarch and ¾ cup (180 ml) of ice water and whisk well. Add more water to the batter, 1 tablespoon (15 ml) at a time, to reach the consistency of the thin batter used for American breakfast pancakes. Add the spinach, onion and shrimp; then, using kitchen tongs, toss well to coat. The batter will coat the spinach lightly.

Heat a heavy skillet over medium heat until hot. Add 1 tablespoon (15 ml) of oil and swirl it around to coat the skillet. Using kitchen tongs, scoop up about a quarter of the spinach mixture and spread it thinly and evenly in the hot skillet to make a pancake about 7 inches (18.5 cm) in diameter. Cook for 3 to 4 minutes, or until the bottom turns deep golden brown.

Flip the pancake to the other side and cook for another 3 minutes, pressing gently with a spatula. Drizzle a little more oil around the edges of the pancake if the skillet becomes dry. The more oil, the crispier the pancake becomes. Adjust the heat so that you don't burn the crust.

Remove the pancake from the skillet and place it on a serving platter. Cook the other pancakes as directed.

While the pancakes cook, prepare the dipping sauce. In a small bowl, combine the soy sauce, lemon juice and chili flakes, if using.

Serve pancakes hot with the dipping sauce.

## BEEF-ASPARAGUS-RICE CAKE SKEWERS

(TTEOKSANJEOK, 떡산적)

**MAKES 10 TO 12 SKEWERS**

1½ lb (680 g) store-bought fresh or chilled rice cake sticks

8 oz (225 g) beef striploin or sirloin

2 tbsp (30 ml) soy sauce

1 tbsp (15 ml) sweet rice wine (mirin)

2 tsp (9 g) sugar

1 tsp sesame oil

1 clove garlic, finely minced

¼ tsp freshly ground black pepper

1 bunch asparagus

1 to 2 tbsp (15 to 30 ml) cooking oil

2 tbsp (18 g) finely chopped pine nuts or walnuts, for garnish

Sanjeok is a well-known holiday food in Korea. A variety of vegetables, meat, rice cakes and even kimchi are strung together on skewers and then panfried. Koreans often coat their sanjeok with egg batter, but this version is great without it. It doesn't need it, and forgoing the batter also makes this even easier and quicker to make. If you don't have access to fresh rice cakes, you can use chilled rice cakes. Both types of rice cake sticks are available in Korean grocery stores. I use asparagus, but you can use green onion, fresh chile, mushrooms, kimchi or anything you can skewer instead.

Soak 12 (5- to 6-inch [12.5- to 15-cm]-long) bamboo skewers in cold water for at least 20 minutes.

Separate the rice cake sticks if they are fresh. If chilled, soak them in warm water for 10 minutes to soften them, then drain.

Cut the beef into ½-inch (1.3-cm)-thick strips that are about ½ inch (1.3 cm) longer than the rice cakes, since they will shrink once cooked.

In a medium bowl, combine the soy sauce, rice wine, sugar, sesame oil, garlic and pepper; mix well. Add the beef and toss to coat. Set aside for 10 minutes.

Cut the asparagus to the same length as the rice cake, trimming away the white fibrous part on the bottom.

Taking care not to poke yourself, thread the rice cakes, beef strips and asparagus one after another onto the bamboo skewers.

In a large skillet, heat a small amount of cooking oil over medium heat. Gently place the skewers in the skillet and panfry them for 1 to 2 minutes on each side, or until the beef is seared and cooked to your preference.

Serve the skewers on a platter, garnished with the chopped nuts. Serve warm.

# (HAEMUL PAJEON, 해물파전)

**MAKES 2 LARGE PANCAKES;
SERVES 6 TO 8**

If you're looking for Korea's famous savory pancakes, look no further. This haemul pajeon is perhaps the most celebrated of Korea's renowned varieties of savory pancakes. This recipe will allow you to mimic what you may have had in your favorite Korean restaurant. Whole green onions are used with a variety of fresh or frozen seafood. You can also specialize with only one type of seafood, if you like. This pancake is large, so if you have a large pancake griddle, that would work the best. If not, trim your green onion to fit in your skillet. I recommend using thin and slender green onions, rather than the large and thick kind.

## PANCAKE BATTER

1 cup (158 g) sweet rice flour

1 cup (125 g) all-purpose flour

2 tbsp (16 g) cornstarch

½ tsp salt

½ tsp sugar

½ tsp garlic or onion powder

2 cups (480 ml) + 2 tbsp (30 ml) ice water

4 tbsp (60 ml) oil, plus more as needed, divided

3 bunches green onions, trimmed

1 lb (455 g) total fresh seafood of your choice, such as shrimp, squid, oysters, clams, etc., cut if needed

3 large eggs, beaten

2 fresh red chiles, sliced (optional)

## DIPPING SAUCE

3 tbsp (45 ml) soy sauce

1 tbsp (6 g) Korean chili flakes

2 tbsp (30 ml) rice vinegar

2 tsp (10 ml) water

1 clove garlic, finely minced

1 tsp sesame oil

1 tsp toasted sesame seeds

## COOK'S TIP:

For convenience, you can use store-bought Korean pancake mix (buchim garu) for the batter. Mix 1 cup (158 g) of sweet rice flour (chapssalgaru) plus 1 cup (120 g) of pancake mix with 2 cups (480 ml) of water. Korean pancake mix is available in your local Asian or Korean market.

For the pancake batter, in a bowl, whisk together the dry ingredients. Add the ice water and mix until it forms a batter.

On a square griddle or in a large skillet, heat 2 tablespoons (30 ml) of the cooking oil over medium heat. Arrange half of the green onions side by side on the griddle. Drizzle ½ to ⅔ cup (120 to 160 ml) of the batter evenly over the green onions. It is okay if the batter doesn't cover the green onions completely.

Layer half of the seafood on top. Drizzle 2 to 3 tablespoons (30 to 45 ml) of the batter on top of the seafood, followed by half of the beaten eggs. If using fresh chiles, scatter half of them on top. Lower the heat to medium-low and let the pancake cook for 3 to 4 minutes. If the skillet seems dry, drizzle more cooking oil around the edges of the pancake. The more oil, the crispier the pancake will be.

When the edge of the batter seems dry and crisp, carefully turn the pancake to the other side, using two large spatulas. The crust should be deep golden brown and crisp. Press the pancake down gently a couple of times with a spatula. Drizzle a little more cooking oil around the pancake again, if needed. Let the pancake sear for another 3 to 4 minutes.

Cover the skillet with a large serving platter and flip it over, turning the pancake out onto the platter. This way, you will get the pancake right side up. Cook the second pancake as directed.

Prepare the dipping sauce. In a small bowl, combine all the sauce ingredients and mix well. Serve the pancakes hot with the dipping sauce.

If preferred, slice the pancakes to your desired size with a pizza cutter or knife before serving. To do that, you will need to slide the pancake onto a cutting board, slice and then put the slices back on the serving platter. Traditionally, the pancakes can be sliced into large chunks, then you can use a pair of chopsticks to tear bite-size pieces off the chunk.

## (YACHAE HOPPANG, 야채호빵)

### MAKES 8 BUNS

Steamed buns are a popular street food that you can find in many old-fashioned markets in Korea. Some are filled with sweet fillings; others, with a variety of savory delights. Since they are steamed, not baked, the texture of the buns is exceptionally soft and moist. Traditionally, pork is the most common filling, but beef or chicken would be wonderful, too. The dough rises more easily if you use instant yeast. If you use active yeast, you will need to proof the yeast in a warm liquid first before adding the dry ingredients.

### DOUGH

2¼ cups (281 g) all-purpose flour, plus more for kneading (optional)

2 tsp (8 g) instant yeast

¾ tsp baking powder

2 tbsp (26 g) sugar

½ tsp salt

½ cup (120 ml) lukewarm water

⅓ cup (80 ml) lukewarm whole milk

1 tbsp (15 ml) cooking oil

Cooking oil spray for rising and liners

### FILLING

4 oz (115 g) sweet potato noodles

1 tbsp (15 ml) cooking oil

½ cup (80 g) finely chopped onion

½ cup (75 g) seeded and finely chopped red bell pepper

8 oz (225 g) ground pork

½ cup (50 g) finely chopped Asian chives or green onion

2 fresh chile peppers, seeded and sliced

1 tbsp (15 ml) soy sauce

1 tbsp (15 ml) oyster sauce

1 tsp sesame oil

¼ tsp freshly ground black pepper

In the bowl of an electric mixer fitted with the whisk attachment, whisk together the flour, yeast, baking powder, sugar and salt. Add the water, milk and oil and stir with a wooden spoon until the mixture comes together. Change to the dough hook and knead the dough for 5 minutes on medium-low speed. Alternatively, if you prefer to use your hands, knead the dough on a lightly floured surface for about 8 minutes.

Divide the dough into 8 pieces and shape them into balls. Place them on an oiled cookie sheet, evenly spaced from one another. Cover it with a piece of oiled plastic wrap. Let the dough balls rise in a warm place to double their volume, for about 1 hour.

Meanwhile, prepare the filling. Bring a pot of water to a boil, add the sweet potato noodles and cook for 5 minutes, stirring occasionally. Drain the noodles in a strainer and rinse them with cold water. Place the noodles on a cutting board and chop them finely, to about ½ inch (1.3 cm) long.

In a skillet, heat the cooking oil over medium heat. Add the onion and bell pepper and cook for 1 minute. Add the pork and cook for 3 to 4 minutes. Add the chives and chile peppers and cook for 1 minute. Add the noodles and season the mixture with the soy sauce, oyster sauce, sesame oil and black pepper; toss well. Remove it from the heat and let it cool.

Flatten 16 paper muffin liners with your hands and spray them with cooking oil; set aside.

When the dough balls are doubled in volume, flatten each ball with your hand to make a disk about 4 inches (10 cm) in diameter. You don't need to make a perfect round shape. Spoon about 2 tablespoons (25 g) of filling onto the center of the flattened dough, fold the edges toward the center and crimp them to seal. Place the buns on the oiled muffin liners. Press down on their tops gently, then cover them with a clean kitchen towel. Let the buns rest for 10 minutes.

In the meantime, place a bamboo or stainless-steel steamer in the base of a large pot, fill the base with water to below the level of the steamer and bring it to a boil. Make sure to wrap the lid with a kitchen towel to collect any water that may drip as you open the lid. Place the buns in the hot steamer, cover and steam them for 10 minutes. Turn off the heat and wait for 3 minutes without opening the lid. This will prevent the buns from sagging down after they are steamed. Serve the buns warm.

**COOK'S TIP:** Leftover japchae (page 89), chopped finely with a knife, is a wonderful filling for these buns.

**( T T E O K P P O K I , 떡볶이 )**

1 lb (455 g) store-bought rice cake sticks, fresh or vacuum-sealed

3 cups (720 ml) water

6 or 7 large dried anchovies, deveined, head removed

1 (6" [15-cm]) piece dried sea kelp

2 tbsp (33 g) Korean chili paste

1 tbsp (6 g) Korean chili flakes

1 tbsp (15 ml) soy sauce

1 tbsp (13 g) sugar

2 tbsp (30 ml) Korean oligo syrup or corn syrup

½ tsp freshly ground black pepper

2 slices flat fish cake, sliced into big bite-size pieces

½ Asian leek or 2 green onions, sliced

**Millions of Korean people have loved Korea's chewy, spicy rice cakes from their childhood. For some reason, soft chewy rice cakes simmered in a spicy and gently sweet chili sauce are irresistible. This dish can be served as a simple meal, since it can fill you up easily. The street vendor–style rice cakes are perhaps the most sought-after kind among all the rice cake recipes out there. Lucky for us, it is easy to replicate them at home. There are many ways to mimic the flavor, but I found the best-tasting ones are the simplest. The anchovy stock is a must. It contributes the underlying flavor of the dish without being fishy.**

If your rice cakes are vacuum-sealed, soak them in cold water for 10 minutes and drain. Rinse the cakes under running water and set them aside. If using fresh cakes, separate each cake and set them aside.

Prepare the anchovy stock. In a deep skillet, combine the water, anchovies and dried sea kelp and bring it to a boil. Lower the heat to low and let it simmer for 3 to 4 minutes. Discard the anchovies and sea kelp.

Add the chili paste, chili flakes, soy sauce, sugar, oligo syrup and black pepper to the skillet and mix well.

Add the rice cakes and fish cakes to the skillet. Stir while bringing them to a boil over medium-high heat. Lower the heat to medium-low, add the leek and continue to simmer for 4 to 5 minutes, or until the sauce thickens to your liking, stirring frequently so the rice cakes don't stick to the bottom of the skillet. Serve hot.

**COOK'S TIP:** Hard-boiled eggs and fried Korean dumplings are popular accompaniments to this rice cake dish among the locals. You can use store-bought Korean dumplings, which are similar to pot stickers or gyoza. Add the eggs and fried dumplings when serving the dish and smother them in the chili sauce to enjoy together. Yummy!

## (MINI JUMUKBAP, 미니주먹밥)

# PICNIC RICE BALLS

## MAKES 14 TO 16 SMALL RICE BALLS EACH

### WATERCRESS-BACON RICE BALLS

4 strips bacon

1 bunch watercress

Salt, to taste

2 tsp (10 ml) Korean soy sauce for soup

1 tsp sesame oil

2 cups (340 g) cooked short-grain white rice

### BEEF RICE BALLS

⅓ lb (150 g) ground beef

2 tbsp (30 ml) soy sauce

1 tbsp (13 g) sugar

2 tsp (10 ml) sesame oil

¼ tsp freshly ground black pepper

2 tsp (10 ml) cooking oil

1 green onion, finely chopped

2 cups (340 g) cooked short-grain white rice

Salt (optional)

### EGG RICE BALLS

2 large eggs, beaten

½ tsp Korean salted shrimp

¼ cup (38 g) seeded and minced red bell pepper

2 tsp (10 ml) cooking oil

2 cups (340 g) cooked short-grain white rice

Salt (optional)

Ever found yourself with a lot of leftover short-grain rice? If you like to eat Asian food, you probably have. This recipe comes to the rescue. These little rice balls are the perfect finger food to fill your picnic baskets, potluck party trays or your kid's lunch box. Long-grain rice won't work because it lacks the stickiness necessary to hold these balls together. The following are three crowd-pleasing ways to create delicious mini rice balls. Use your imagination with whatever you have in your kitchen. Try making these rice balls small, around golf ball size, so that you can pop them into your mouth whole. Or make them the size of tennis balls if you need to serve someone annoying. Just whisper in their ear a reminder that consuming these in multiple bites is not allowed in Korean etiquette.

**For watercress bacon rice balls,** in a skillet, cook the bacon until crisp. Chop it finely and set it aside.

Bring a pot of water to a boil, add the watercress along with some salt and blanch until it's soft, 1 to 2 minutes. Drain the watercress and rinse it under cold running water. Squeeze it to remove any excess water. Chop the watercress finely, place it in a large mixing bowl and season it with the Korean soy sauce for soup and sesame oil. Toss well.

Add the cooked rice and chopped bacon to the watercress and mix well. Taste and season with salt, if needed. With fingers coated with a bit of oil so the rice won't stick to them, form portions of the rice mixture into golf ball–size balls, compressing well so that they hold together.

**For beef rice balls,** in a bowl, combine the beef, soy sauce, sugar, sesame oil and black pepper; mix well. In a small skillet, heat the cooking oil over medium-high heat. Add the beef mixture and cook until it is done and crisp, 3 to 4 minutes. Transfer the hot beef to a bowl, add the green onion and rice and mix well. Taste and season it with salt, if needed. With fingers coated with a bit of oil so the rice won't stick to them, form portions of the rice mixture into golf ball–size balls, compressing well so that they hold together.

**For egg rice balls,** in a bowl, combine the beaten egg, salted shrimp and bell pepper. In a skillet, heat the oil over medium-low heat. Pour the egg mixture into the skillet and scramble the mixture with a pair of chopsticks or a fork until it's fully cooked. Transfer the cooked egg mixture to a bowl, add the rice and mix well. Taste and season it with salt, if needed. With fingers coated with a bit of oil so the rice won't stick to them, form portions of the rice mixture into golf ball–size balls, compressing well so that they hold together.

**COOK'S TIP:** I found it is easier to form the rice into balls if you wear disposable plastic gloves, rather than using bare hands. Dab them with a little bit of oil and form the rice to make a ball.

## (KIMCHI GULIM MANDU, 김치굴림만두)

1 lb (455 g) minced pork

1¼ cups (313 g) finely chopped sour cabbage kimchi (page 146), squeezed to remove moisture

2 green onions, finely chopped

1 clove garlic, minced

1 tbsp (15 ml) soy sauce

1½ tsp (8 ml) oyster sauce

1½ tsp (8 ml) sesame oil

½ tsp sugar

¼ tsp freshly ground black pepper

1½ cups (192 g) potato starch or cornstarch, for coating

About 3 cups (720 ml) chicken broth or anchovy broth, to keep the dumplings moist

### DIPPING SAUCE

3 tbsp (45 ml) soy sauce

1½ tbsp (23 ml) rice vinegar

1½ tbsp (10 g) Korean chili flakes (optional)

# KIMCHI NUDE DUMPLINGS
## MAKES 20 TO 24 DUMPLING BALLS

**Kimchi brings a flavorful kick and crunch to these dumplings. Why are they "nude"? Because these dumplings are not covered with traditional wrappers. Instead, they are coated with potato starch or cornstarch to hold the filling inside. They become translucent once cooked, revealing their inner beauty. Scandalous! Using potato starch will yield more translucency than cornstarch. These little dumplings are a lot easier and quicker to make than the traditional kind. They are perfect for those avoiding gluten in their diet as well. But remember, if you want the recipe to be completely gluten-free, make sure that the soy sauce, oyster sauce and kimchi are all gluten-free.**

In a large bowl, combine the pork, kimchi, green onions, garlic, soy sauce, oyster sauce, sesame oil, sugar and black pepper and mix well with your hands. Roll the mixture into balls about 1¼ inches (3 cm) in diameter.

Place the potato starch in a large, shallow bowl. Roll the dumpling balls to coat them evenly with the starch. When you finish coating the entire batch of dumpling balls, repeat the coating again so that you are coating them at least twice.

Bring a large pot of water to a gentle boil over medium heat. Drop in the dumpling balls, a few at a time, and let them simmer for about 3 minutes, stirring occasionally so that they don't stick to the bottom of the pot. When the balls float to the top, they are done.

Meanwhile, in a saucepan, heat the broth over low heat. As the dumpling balls finish cooking, transfer them to the warm broth where they will be kept warm.

In a small bowl, combine all the sauce ingredients and mix well. Serve the dumplings warm with the dipping sauce.

**COOK'S TIP:** For this recipe, it is important to remove extra moisture from the cabbage kimchi. Remove any stuffing from your kimchi before you chop, then squeeze out the juice. If you prefer less spicy dumpling balls, rinse the cabbage kimchi in running water to get rid of the chili coating before chopping. Again, be sure to squeeze out the excess moisture before using in this recipe.

## (SALAD KIMBAP, 샐러드김밥)

4 cups (680 g) cooked short-grain white rice, hot or warm

1 tsp salt, divided

2 tbsp (30 ml) Korean plum extract

2 tsp (10 ml) cooking oil

4 large eggs, beaten with ¼ tsp salt

4 slices thick bacon, or 8 slices thin bacon

1 English cucumber

4 dried seaweed sheets (gim or sushi nori)

8 green lettuce leaves

3 cups (210 g) thinly shredded red cabbage

1 large carrot, thinly shredded

### DIPPING SAUCE

3 tbsp (45 ml) soy sauce

1 tbsp (15 ml) water

2 tsp (9 g) sugar

2 tsp (10 g) prepared Korean yellow mustard or Dijon mustard

1 tbsp (15 ml) rice vinegar

# SEAWEED SALAD RICE ROLLS
## MAKES 4 LARGE ROLLS

Unlike the traditional Korean seaweed rice rolls (gimbap), these salad rice rolls are easier and quicker to prepare. The only things you need to cook are eggs and bacon. Stuffed with fresh lettuce, cucumber, carrot and cabbage, these rolls are like eating a salad wrapped in rice and seaweed. What really sets these apart is the dipping sauce. You will love the gentle kick from the Korean mustard! Since these rolls travel well, they are perfect for picnics or potluck parties—that's what Korean seaweed rice rolls are famous for.

Put the cooked rice in a wooden mixing bowl. Add ½ teaspoon of the salt and the Korean plum extract and mix well with a rice paddle. Cover it with a damp, clean towel and set aside.

In a nonstick skillet, heat the oil over medium heat. Pour in the beaten eggs and cook for 1 to 2 minutes. Turn them to the other side and cook for another 30 seconds, or until they're fully cooked. Turn out the cooked eggs onto a cutting board and let them cool for 2 minutes. Then, fold them a couple of times and slice them into thin strips; set aside.

Cook the bacon until it's crisp yet soft, 2 to 3 minutes; set aside.

Cut the cucumber in half lengthwise. Scoop out the seeds with a spoon and discard them, then slice the cucumber thinly on the diagonal. Put the cucumber slices in a bowl and sprinkle the remaining ½ teaspoon of salt over them; mix well and let them sit for 5 minutes. Squeeze the cucumber pieces to remove the extra moisture; set aside.

To assemble the rolls, place a bamboo sushi roll on a cutting board and lay a sheet of seaweed on top. Put 1 cup (170 g) of the rice on the seaweed sheet and spread it evenly to cover the seaweed sheet, leaving about 1 inch (2.5 cm) uncovered on one end. Place 1 or 2 lettuce leaves on top of the rice, flattening the leaf down. Layer it with about a quarter of your egg strips, 1 bacon strip (or 2 if thin), and some cucumber, cabbage and carrot over the lettuce. From the edge of the seaweed on your side, start rolling the bamboo roll to wrap everything firmly and tightly inside the seaweed. The lettuce should surround all the other salad ingredients. Unroll the bamboo roll and set the seaweed rice roll aside. Repeat to finish the rest of rolls.

In a small bowl, combine all the sauce ingredients and mix well.

Cut each seaweed rice roll to about ¾-inch (2-cm) thickness with a slightly wet, sharp knife. Arrange them on a serving platter and serve with the dipping sauce.

**COOK'S TIP:** If you don't have Korean plum extract, you can use a mixture of 2 tablespoons (30 ml) of rice vinegar and 1 tablespoon (13 g) of sugar as a substitute. Make sure the sugar is completely dissolved. Microwave the mixture for 10 to 15 seconds, if needed, to help dissolve the sugar.

# THE MAIN
## EVENT

**WHETHER** it is beef, pork, chicken or seafood, Korean cuisine has its unique flavors that are different than other Asian cuisines.

By using a variety of fermented condiments, such as soy sauce, fish sauce, soybean paste and chili paste to season the meat or seafood, Korean chefs bring forth robust and earthy flavors that many people love. It is no wonder that Korean cuisine is becoming more and more popular worldwide.

In this chapter, you will find some of the most sought-after authentic Korean main dishes from different regions of Korea. You can enjoy the most popular Korean beef made in Seoul style (page 36) and the pork dish called mackjeok (page 51) that ancient royals enjoyed. You can fearlessly make authentic Korean cuisine at home once you know a few cooking tips. The only dilemma will be which dish in this chapter to make first.

## (BULGOGI, 불고기)

# CLASSIC KOREAN BEEF
## SERVES 4 TO 6

1 large Korean pear, peeled

6 tbsp (90 ml) soy sauce

1 tbsp (15 ml) Korean tuna sauce or Korean soy sauce for soup

2 tbsp (26 g) sugar

¼ cup (60 ml) Korean oligo syrup or corn syrup

3 cloves garlic, finely minced

½ tsp freshly ground black pepper

1 cup (240 ml) water

21 oz (600 g) very thinly sliced beef sirloin, thawed if frozen

1 medium onion, sliced

5 oz (140 g) enoki or sliced button mushrooms

10 oz (280 g) bok choy, quartered (optional)

2 green onions, thinly sliced diagonally

2 tsp (10 ml) sesame oil

Cooked rice, for serving

Every region in Korea has its unique way of making the famous Korean beef known as bulgogi. Some grill their bulgogi over an open flame, using a grill mesh, whereas others stir-fry their bulgogi in a skillet. Some people love their bulgogi crisp; others prefer it moist with juicy gravy to soak into their rice. This simple recipe is close to the old-fashioned Seoul-style bulgogi with tender beef and mushrooms in a flavorful soy sauce and pear broth. The nice thing is you only need 20 minutes of marinating time and just a few minutes to cook. Traditional Seoul-style bulgogi needs a special bulgogi pan that allows you to cook the meat and broth separately at the same time, but you can still cook this at home with just a skillet. I like to add some bok choy to make it heartier. Drizzle the broth over the rice to soak up all the deliciousness and you will taste the ultimate classic Korean beef within 30 minutes, in Seoul style!

Put a large fine-mesh strainer or sieve over a large bowl. Grate the pear on a fine cheese grater over the strainer to catch all the pulp. Grate until you reach the core of the pear. Discard the seeds.

Using the back of a wooden spoon, press the grated pear pulp firmly through the strainer to collect the fresh pear juice. You will get about 1 cup (240 ml) of juice. Discard any pulp that remains in the strainer.

Add the soy sauce, tuna sauce, sugar, syrup, garlic, pepper and water to the pear juice and mix well until the sugar dissolves, 30 to 60 seconds. Add the beef, separating each slice, and the onion to the mixture, then toss with your hands to help the meat soak up the marinade. Let it sit on the counter for 20 minutes.

Heat a large, deep skillet over medium-high heat until hot. Add the beef, onion and the marinade along with the mushrooms and bok choy, if using. Gently stir everything in the skillet and cook until the beef is browned, 2 to 3 minutes.

Add the green onions and drizzle the sesame oil on the beef; toss gently. Serve immediately with rice. Don't forget to drizzle some of the broth over your rice to soak up that wonderful flavor. Any kind of kimchi would be a nice accompaniment.

**COOK'S TIP:** If you like Korean sweet potato noodles (dangmyun), try them with this classic bulgogi. Soak 3½ ounces (100 g) of sweet potato noodles in hot water for 20 minutes. Drain and rinse the noodles a couple of times in a strainer. Cut the noodles, if needed. Then, add the noodles to the hot skillet along with the beef and mushrooms to cook together.

**(TTEOKGALBI, 떡갈비)**

# SOUTHERN-STYLE BEEF RIB PATTIES
## MAKES 6 TO 8 PATTIES

### PATTIES

17.5 oz (500 g) beef rib meat or sirloin, or combination of both, diced

½ medium onion, finely minced

1 Asian leek, white part only, finely minced

¼ cup (36 g) sweet rice flour

3 cloves garlic, finely minced

¼ cup (35 g) finely chopped pine nuts or walnuts, plus more for garnish (optional)

2 tbsp (30 ml) soy sauce

½ tsp salt

¾ tsp freshly ground black pepper

1 tbsp (15 g) light brown sugar

2 tsp (10 ml) sesame oil

2 tbsp (30 ml) cooking oil

Alfalfa sprouts, for garnish (optional)

### HONEY GLAZE

3 tbsp (63 g) honey

2 tbsp (30 ml) soy sauce

1 tbsp (15 ml) sesame oil

Cooked rice, for serving

If you want to impress your guests with Korean-style beef, try these patties that are often served in upscale Korean restaurants. The delicious honey glaze makes them sparkle and look very elegant. If you have a food processor and an electric mixer, this will be a piece of cake to make. If not, you will need to chop your meat into small pieces with your knife and use some elbow grease to knead it. Substituting ground or minced beef won't bring the same texture; you will lose the true taste of these delicious patties. As my father-in-law often said, "If it's worth doing, it's worth doing right." Traditionally rib meats are used for these patties, but you can use other tender cuts of beef, or a combination.

To prepare the patties, place the diced beef in a food processor and pulse a few times until you get small but coarse pieces slightly larger than ground beef. It is okay to have a few pieces that are bigger than the others.

Transfer the beef to the bowl of an electric mixer and add all the patty ingredients, except the cooking oil and garnishes, and stir briefly with a wooden spoon to combine. Then, using the paddle attachment, mix at high speed for 2 minutes, or until the mixture becomes very sticky and all the ingredients are well incorporated.

Divide the meat mixture into 6 to 8 portions (or any other size you desire) and shape it into patties. Set aside.

In a large skillet, heat 1 tablespoon (15 ml) of the cooking oil over medium heat. Place the patties in the skillet and cook until they're browned, 2 to 3 minutes. Flip them to the other side and continue to cook for another 2 minutes, or until completely cooked, adding a little more oil if needed and adjusting the heat so the patties do not burn.

Meanwhile, prepare the glaze. In a small bowl, combine the honey, soy sauce and sesame oil. Drizzle the glaze over the beef while it's still in the skillet and let it sizzle for 10 seconds.

Transfer the patties to a serving plate and garnish with alfalfa sprouts or pine nuts, if desired. Serve hot with rice.

**COOK'S TIP:** If you don't have a food processor and stand mixer, you can slice the beef very thinly with your knife, then pound the meat with the dull edge of your knife several times to tenderize the meat. Slice the meat a few times more to make smaller pieces. Collect them in a bowl and add the rest of the ingredients, except the cooking oil and garnishes. Knead the meat mixture for 5 to 10 minutes, until it becomes sticky.

# L.A.-STYLE BEEF BBQ RIBS
## SERVES 6 TO 8

**(L.A. GALBI, LA 갈비)**

24 oz (720 ml) sweet carbonated drink, such as cola

3½ lb (1.6 kg) beef short ribs

1 Korean pear, peeled, seeded and diced

1 medium onion, diced

3 to 4 cloves garlic

½ cup (120 ml) water

¾ cup (180 ml) soy sauce

½ cup (113 g) light brown sugar

1 tsp pureed fresh ginger

3 tbsp (45 ml) sweet rice wine (mirin)

1 tbsp (15 ml) sesame oil

1 tsp freshly ground black pepper

2 tbsp (18 g) finely chopped pine nuts or walnuts, for garnish

Cooked rice, for serving

Lettuce, for serving (optional)

Korean seasoned soybean paste, for serving (optional)

Unlike the labor-intensive traditional Korean barbecued beef ribs that require you to butterfly the rib meat with a knife, L.A.-style ribs are cut at lateral angles with an electric slicer displaying the three rib bone eyes. The name L.A. galbi was originated by Korean immigrants in the Los Angeles area who started cutting the bones along the long edge, which enables the marinade to penetrate into the meat faster. To maximize the tenderness and juiciness of the ribs, try soaking them in a sweet carbonated drink for 30 minutes prior to marinating them. It does not dissolve the meat, but the acidity of the soda does help tenderize it, making your Korean ribs extra soft and very flavorful.

In a large bowl, pour the carbonated drink over the ribs and let them soak for 30 minutes. Drain the ribs and set aside.

In a blender, process the pear, onion, garlic and water together until smooth. Pour the pear puree into a fine sieve placed over a large bowl. Press the puree firmly with the back of a wooden spoon to collect the juice and discard the fibrous pulp remaining in the sieve.

Add the soy sauce, brown sugar, ginger, rice wine, sesame oil and pepper to the bowl and whisk well until the sugar is dissolved.

Add the ribs to the sauce mixture and coat them well. Let the ribs marinate, covered, in the refrigerator for 8 to 10 hours.

Grill the ribs on a hot charcoal or electric grill for 2 to 3 minutes on each side, or panfry them in a hot skillet. Garnish with the pine nuts and serve warm with rice, lettuce and Korean seasoned soybean paste as a topping sauce, if desired.

## (SOGOGI CHAPSSALGUI, 소고기찹쌀구이)

½ large Korean pear, or 1 Bosc pear, peeled and seeded

1 lb (455 g) thinly sliced beef eye round (sliced about ⅛" [3-mm] thick)

3 tbsp (45 ml) soy sauce

2 tbsp (42 g) honey

2 tsp (10 ml) sesame oil

1 tbsp (10 g) finely minced garlic

1 tbsp (15 ml) sweet rice wine (mirin)

½ tsp freshly ground black pepper

½ cup (60 g) very finely chopped walnuts

1 cup (158 g) sweet rice flour

Cooking oil, for panfrying, as needed

3 oz (85 g) spring salad greens, for serving

¼ head iceberg lettuce, torn into large chunks, for serving

3 to 4 young pink radishes, sliced into thin strips, for serving

5 to 6 perilla or fresh mint leaves, sliced into thin strips, for serving

### CITRON DRESSING

¼ cup (60 ml) store-bought Korean citron tea

2 tbsp (30 ml) fresh lemon juice

2 tbsp (30 ml) salad oil

1 tbsp (16 g) whole-grain mustard

2 tbsp (30 ml) water

Pinch of salt

# CRISPY BEEF SALAD WITH CITRON DRESSING
## SERVES 4 TO 8

This elegant beef salad is usually served at a party where you want to impress someone. Thin slices of beef are encrusted with finely chopped walnuts and then lightly coated with sweet rice flour before they are panfried to perfection. Served with fragrant Korean citron dressing, this beautiful salad is sure to amaze your guests. Don't fear the long list of ingredients. The salad comes together quite easily.

Grate the pear with a fine cheese grater into a bowl. Add the beef slices and mix together; let it marinate for 20 minutes.

In another large bowl, combine the soy sauce, honey, sesame oil, garlic, rice wine and pepper. Remove the beef from the pear marinade and add it to the soy sauce mixture. Discard the pear marinade. Toss it well to coat. Add the walnuts and toss well.

Put the sweet rice flour into a shallow bowl. Take a slice of beef with some walnuts attached to the surface. Spread the beef flat on the rice flour and very gently press it down with your fingers to lightly coat the meat. Turn it to the other side and coat again lightly. Gently shake off any extra flour, being careful not to shake off the walnuts.

In a nonstick skillet, heat about 1 tablespoon (15 ml) of oil over medium heat. Add the beef, a few slices at a time, and panfry them for about 2 minutes on each side, or until they're golden brown and crisp, drizzling in more oil if the skillet seems dry. Repeat with the rest of the beef slices, adjusting the heat level and adding oil as needed so that you don't burn the coating.

In a small bowl, whisk together all the dressing ingredients; set aside or chill until ready to use.

Arrange the beef slices on a large serving platter. Top them with the salad greens, lettuce, radishes and perilla. Just before serving, drizzle the salad with the citron dressing and serve immediately. This is best served when the beef is still warm.

**COOK'S TIP:** Korean citron tea (yujacha) is a popular winter tea made with citron fruit (similar to lemon) and honey or sugar. A jar of Korean citron tea is easily found in any Korean grocery store. I often see it in wholesale grocery stores in the United States, too. If you can't find it, the best substitute would be an equal amount of orange marmalade.

**(DOEJI GALBIJJIM, 돼지갈비찜)**

# PORK RIBS WITH GARLIC, PEAR & JUJUBE
## SERVES 4

2½ lb (1.1 kg) pork short ribs

1 large Korean pear, peeled, seeded and diced

½ large onion, diced

¼ cup (60 ml) soy sauce

3 tbsp (45 ml) sweet rice wine (mirin)

1 tsp pureed fresh ginger

2 tbsp (30 ml) Korean plum extract or corn syrup

½ tsp freshly ground black pepper

2 tbsp (30 ml) cooking oil

8 to 10 cloves garlic, thinly sliced

5 or 6 dried jujubes

2 tbsp (13 g) thinly sliced fresh ginger, for garnish

1 green onion, finely chopped, for garnish

1 tbsp (8 g) toasted sesame seeds, for garnish

Cooked rice, for serving

Sweetened with natural sugars from the Korean pear and dried jujube, these pork ribs are succulent treasures. The enzyme in the pear—which often seems to be Korean cuisine's secret ingredient—will tenderize the meat dramatically. Korean pears are easily found in the fall and winter seasons in most Korean grocery stores, and it's worth the effort to look for them. The fragrant jujube is the other secret to making these ribs exceptionally delicious. Don't neglect to garnish the ribs with crisp garlic slices. Although this recipe has an extra step of parboiling the ribs first, doing so will help remove a large amount of fat from the ribs.

Put the pork ribs into a large pot and pour in enough water to cover them. Bring the water to a boil over high heat and cook, uncovered, for 3 to 4 minutes. Remove the ribs from the pot and rinse them with hot water; set aside. Discard the cooking liquid.

In a blender, puree the pear and onion until smooth, adding a little water, if needed, to help the blade run. Place a fine sieve over a large bowl and pour the pear puree into the sieve. Press down with the back of a wooden spoon to collect the juice. Discard the fibrous pulp remaining in the sieve. You should be able to collect about 1½ cups (360 ml) of juice.

Add the soy sauce, rice wine, ginger puree, plum extract and pepper to the pear juice to make a sauce; stir well and set aside.

In a large, deep, lidded skillet or wok, heat the oil over medium-low heat, add the garlic slices and fry them until they turn light golden brown and crisp, 2 to 3 minutes, being careful not to burn them, adjusting the heat level, if needed. Remove the skillet from the heat and, leaving the garlic-infused oil in the pan, transfer the fried garlic slices to a paper towel–lined plate; set aside.

Return the skillet to medium-high heat and add the pork ribs; stir-fry them for 1 minute. Add the sauce and the dried jujubes to the skillet; mix well and let the mixture come to a boil. Lower the heat to medium-low and simmer, covered, for 20 minutes.

Uncover the skillet and increase the heat to high. Bring the sauce to a boil again and let it thicken until it attains a very thick, glazelike consistency, tossing the ribs occasionally, about 5 minutes.

Put the glazed ribs on a serving platter and garnish with the sliced ginger, green onion, sesame seeds and fried garlic slices. Serve hot with rice.

## (BOSSAM, 보쌈)

# BRAISED PORK BELLY WITH SPICY RADISH SALAD

## SERVES 4 TO 6

### RADISH SALAD

1½ lb (680 g) Korean radish, peeled and cut into ¼" (6-mm)-thick matchsticks

1 tbsp (18 g) salt

2 tbsp (26 g) sugar

2 to 3 tbsp (13 to 19 g) Korean chili flakes

3 cloves garlic, finely minced

1 tsp pureed fresh ginger

1 tbsp (13 g) Korean salted shrimp, minced

2 green onions, chopped

1 tbsp (15 ml) Korean plum extract (optional)

2 tbsp (30 ml) Korean oligo syrup or corn syrup

1 tbsp (8 g) roasted sesame seeds

### PORK BELLY

6 to 8 cups (1.4 to 1.9 L) water

1 Asian leek or large onion, cut in half or quartered

8 cloves garlic

3 bay leaves

10 whole peppercorns

4 slices fresh ginger

1 sweet apple, cut in half

2 tbsp (33 g) Korean fermented soybean paste

2 lb (905 g) fresh pork belly

Assorted lettuce leaves, for serving

Korean salted shrimp, for serving

Bossam is a dish for pork lovers. The combination of juicy, tender pork belly slices and a spicy, crunchy radish salad provides a fantastic flavor explosion. The key to making good bossam is in how you braise the pork to avoid the gamey odor while still retaining its moistness and tenderness. With this recipe, you will get the best juicy, tender pork you will ever have. Try it with freshly made cabbage kimchi (page 146). It's divine!

For the radish salad, put the radish matchsticks in a large bowl and sprinkle them with the salt and sugar. Toss well and let them sit for 30 minutes. The radishes will release some moisture. Drain the liquid and squeeze the radishes to remove the extra moisture.

Transfer the radishes to another large bowl and add the rest of the salad ingredients; toss well to coat them. Taste and adjust the seasoning according to your taste. Chill the salad until ready to serve.

Meanwhile, prepare the pork belly. Pour the water into a large, lidded pot and add the leek, garlic, bay leaves, peppercorns, ginger, apple and soybean paste. The liquid should be deep enough to cover the pork. Add more water, if needed. Bring the liquid to a full boil over high heat.

Add the pork belly to the pot, cutting it to fit if it's too big. When the liquid comes back to a boil, lower the heat to medium-low. Cover it and simmer for 40 to 50 minutes, or until the pork is tender.

Remove the pork belly from the braising liquid and let it cool for 5 minutes. Slice the pork to your desired thickness and arrange it on a serving platter. Serve with the radish salad, lettuce and salted shrimp.

**COOK'S TIP:** To serve bossam, place a slice of pork belly on a lettuce leaf, dot with a tiny bit of salted shrimp and top with a small amount of radish salad. Put the whole wrap in your mouth and you'll be in heaven!

## (JEYUK BOKKEUM, 제육볶음)

## SPICY PORK STIR-FRY

### SERVES 4

21 oz (600 g) thinly sliced pork shoulder or pork butt

1 tbsp (15 ml) soy sauce

¼ cup (66 g) Korean chili paste

1 to 2 tbsp (6 to 12 g) Korean chili flakes

2 to 3 tbsp (42 to 63 g) honey

1 tbsp (10 g) minced garlic

1 tsp pureed fresh ginger

2 tbsp (30 ml) sweet rice wine (mirin)

1 tbsp (15 ml) sesame oil

Freshly ground black pepper

1 tbsp (15 ml) cooking oil

1 medium onion, sliced

1 fresh green chile, sliced (optional)

1 green onion, sliced

Sesame seeds

Cooked rice, for serving

Lettuce leaves, for serving

This spicy Korean pork stir-fry is perhaps the most popular Korean pork dish. Although it may look scary hot, in reality it is only mildly spicy. You can adjust the heat level by adjusting the amount of chili paste and flakes. The gentle sweetness of the chili sauce goes really well with pork. I highly recommend using thin slices of pork shoulder or pork butt, rather than pork belly or loin; pork belly has too much fat and pork loin is too lean. You can find presliced frozen pork shoulder in many Korean groceries. This is a quick and easy pork stir-fry that anyone can make with great success. So yummy!

Make sure to drain away any liquid coming out of the pork if you thaw it from frozen. Place the pork in a large bowl.

In a small bowl, combine the soy sauce, chili paste, chili flakes, honey, garlic, ginger, rice wine, sesame oil and black pepper; mix well.

Pour the sauce over the pork and mix it together with your hands as if you are massaging the pork, to ensure the sauce infuses every piece of pork.

In a large, heavy-bottomed skillet, heat the cooking oil over medium-high heat until it's very hot. Cooking in batches, if necessary, add the pork, onion and chile, if using, to the skillet. You should hear the loud sizzling sound immediately. Do not overcrowd the skillet. Stir-fry the pork and onion until they are fully cooked, 3 to 4 minutes.

Sprinkle the green onion and sesame seeds on top. Serve hot with rice and lettuce to wrap the pork.

**(MACKJEOK, 맥적)**

2 tbsp (33 g) Korean fermented soybean paste

1 tbsp (15 ml) Korean soy sauce for soup

1 tbsp (21 g) honey

2 tbsp (30 ml) sweet rice wine (mirin)

2 cloves garlic, finely minced

1 tsp pureed fresh ginger

2 tsp (10 ml) sesame oil

Freshly ground black pepper

17.5 oz (500 g) thinly sliced pork shoulder

6½ tbsp (40 g) chopped Asian chives or green onion

Bibb or green leaf lettuce, for serving

## ONION SALAD (PACHAE) (OPTIONAL)

2 large Asian leeks, or 4 green onions

2 tsp (10 ml) soy sauce

2 tsp (4 g) Korean chili flakes

1 tsp sugar

1 tsp cider vinegar

1 tsp sesame oil

2 tsp (5 g) toasted sesame seeds

**COOK'S TIP:** If slicing the leeks or green onions thinly drives you insane, try serving this royal pork with fresh cilantro kimchi (page 154) instead. The gentle fragrance of the cilantro goes really well with this royal pork.

# ANCIENT GRILLED ROYAL PORK
## SERVES 3

*Mackjeok* is an ancient term referring to grilled meat and it is widely believed that the ancient Korean royals enjoyed this dish. It sounds good no matter what era you live in: thinly sliced pork marinated in Korean fermented soybean paste (doenjang) then grilled.

No grill? No problem! You can cook it under the broiler of your oven, or even panfry it, for excellent results. Make sure to get thinly sliced pork shoulder, which is easily found in the frozen section of Korean grocery stores. Otherwise, you might need to bribe your regular butcher to slice it very thinly for you.

In a large bowl, mix together the soybean paste, soy sauce, honey, rice wine, garlic, ginger, sesame oil and a few pinches of black pepper.

Add the pork slices, separating each slice, and the chives. Mix well with your hands, tossing and kneading the meat to ensure all the seasoning is evenly incorporated into the pork. Cover and marinate it for at least 30 minutes, or chill in the fridge for several hours, but no more than 24 hours.

**To cook under the broiler**, adjust the oven rack to 6 inches (15 cm) below the heat source and turn on the broiler. On a large, rimmed cookie sheet, evenly spread out the meat without overcrowding. You might need to cook it in two batches.

Broil the pork for 3 to 4 minutes on one side. Remove the cookie sheet from the oven and turn the meat to the other side; broil again for another 3 minutes, or until some brown spots appear on the surface. Brush the meat with the pan juices remaining on the cookie sheet, to enhance the shine and moisture. Transfer it to a serving dish.

**To panfry on the stovetop**, heat a skillet over medium-high heat until it's very hot and add a little bit of cooking oil. Add the pork and let it sizzle for 1 minute, then stir-fry it until the pork is fully cooked. You will need to cook this in batches if the skillet is not big enough. Transfer it to a serving dish.

For the onion salad, cut the leeks in half lengthwise and remove any hard core from the white stem. Cut it into pieces 3 inches (7.5 cm) long, then slice it very thinly lengthwise and soak it in cold water (it will curl up) and drain. To prepare the dressing, in a small bowl, mix together the rest of the salad ingredients and set aside. Drizzle the dressing over the sliced leeks or toss it together right before you serve it alongside the cooked pork.

To serve, place the pork on the lettuce and top with a bit of the onion salad. Wrap or fold it and enjoy with rice on the side. You can also enjoy this dish family style without lettuce. Just top the pork with the onion salad and serve with rice.

## (TANGSUYUK, 탕수육)

# KOREAN SWEET & SOUR PORK
## SERVES 4 TO 6

1 lb (455 g) pork loin, sliced into
½" (1.3-cm)-thick strips

1 tbsp (15 ml) sweet rice wine (mirin)

½ tsp salt

½ tsp pureed fresh ginger

½ tsp freshly ground black pepper

### BATTER

¾ cup (96 g) potato starch

¼ cup (32 g) cornstarch

½ cup (120 ml) + 1 to 2 tbsp (15 to 30 ml)
water

2 tbsp (30 ml) cooking oil

Peanut oil, for deep-frying

### SAUCE

1½ cups (360 ml) + 3 tbsp (45 ml) water,
divided

7 tbsp (91 g) sugar

1 tbsp (15 ml) soy sauce

¼ cup (60 ml) white vinegar

¼ tsp salt

3 tbsp (24 g) potato starch

½ medium onion, diced

½ red bell pepper, diced

1.5 oz (45 g) fresh wood ear mushrooms
(optional)

½ English cucumber, diced

**COOK'S TIP:** You can
prepare the pork in advance up to and
including the first deep-frying and keep
it in the fridge until a few minutes before
serving. Mix the sauce ingredients ahead of
time and cook the sauce at the last minutes
as well. When the time comes, just reheat
the oil again and do the deep-frying for the
second time. It might take a little longer to
fry because the pork was chilled, but you
will get an even crispier texture.

Most people are aware of Chinese sweet-and-sour dishes, but not everyone knows that Korea boasts its own style of "Chinese" sweet-and-sour pork. The tender, crispy pork covered with a slightly tangy, sweet sauce is by far the most popular dish from Korean-Chinese restaurants. To create the spectacular crisp-yet-chewy texture of the pork, use a combination of potato starch and cornstarch. Deep-frying the pork twice is another key to the crisp texture. Although it would be more convenient to order this dish from a restaurant, this homemade version is healthier and equally tasty. Trust me, it's worth the effort to satisfy your craving for Korean-style sweet-and-sour pork by making this dish yourself.

In a bowl, combine the pork, rice wine, salt, ginger and black pepper; toss well and set it aside for 10 minutes.

In a separate large bowl, mix together the potato starch, cornstarch, ½ cup (120 ml) of the water and the cooking oil. If the batter feels too stiff, stir in more water, 1 tablespoon (15 ml) at a time, to achieve a consistency like sweetened condensed milk. Add the pork to the batter and toss well to coat it.

In a deep skillet or wok, heat peanut oil to 350°F (175°C). A few pieces at a time, slide the pork into the hot oil and deep-fry it for 2 to 3 minutes. Remember that you will be deep-frying the pork again a second time, so don't overcook it the first time. Using a mesh strainer, collect the pork and shake off the excess oil. Transfer the pork to a wire rack or a large paper towel–lined plate. Deep-fry the rest of pork and let it rest on the rack or lined plate for 5 minutes. Reserve the deep-frying oil.

For the sauce, in a small bowl, combine 1½ cups (360 ml) of the water and the sugar, soy sauce, vinegar and salt and whisk well to dissolve the sugar; set aside. In a second small bowl, combine the potato starch and the remaining 3 tablespoons (45 g) of water and mix well; set aside.

In a skillet over high heat, heat 1 tablespoon (15 ml) of the reserved deep-frying oil. Sauté the onion, bell pepper and mushrooms, if using, for 1 minute. Add the cucumber and toss for 10 seconds. Pour in the sauce mixture and let it come to a boil. Add about two-thirds of the starch water and let it thicken. Add more starch water if you desire a thicker sauce consistency. Lower the heat to a simmer to keep the sauce warm while preparing to deep-fry the pork again.

Heat the reserved deep-frying oil again and deep-fry the pork for the second time, 2 to 3 minutes, or until the pieces turn golden brown and crisp. Shake off the excess oil from the pork and place the pork pieces on a serving platter. Pour the sauce over the pork and serve immediately.

## (DAKGALBI, 닭갈비)

# CHUNCHEON-STYLE SPICY CHICKEN STIR-FRY

## SERVES 4

8 oz (225 g) Korean rice cake sticks

1 lb (455 g) boneless, skinless chicken thighs, diced

2 tbsp (30 ml) cooking oil

1 medium onion, sliced

½ small cabbage (about 13 oz [360 g]), diced

1 medium sweet potato (preferably Korean), cut into thin wedges

7 to 9 fresh perilla or basil leaves, sliced

¼ cup (60 ml) cola or chicken stock

1 small Asian leek, or 2 green onions, sliced

1 tbsp (8 g) toasted sesame seeds

### SAUCE

3 tbsp (49 g) Korean chili paste

2 to 3 tbsp (12 to 18 g) Korean chili flakes

3 tbsp (45 ml) soy sauce

2 cloves garlic, minced

1 tbsp (13 g) sugar

2 tsp (4 g) curry powder

2 tbsp (30 ml) sweet rice wine (mirin)

2 tsp (10 ml) sesame oil

½ tsp freshly ground black pepper

2 tbsp (30 ml) Korean oligo syrup or corn syrup (optional)

Dakgalbi originated from the city of Chuncheon in the northeastern part of South Korea in the 1960s. You will still find many restaurants on the busy market streets in Chuncheon claiming that their dakgalbi is the original version. Although *dak* means "chicken," and *galbi* mean "rib," dakgalbi has nothing to do with chicken ribs. Restaurants in Korea serve their dakgalbi on a large hot griddle that is permanently built into the middle of a table, where they stir-fry the dish right before your eyes. Here is a simplified version of the famous Korean chicken stir-fry that you can enjoy at home without drilling a hole in the middle of your dining table.

Soak the rice cakes in warm water for 10 minutes. If the rice cakes are fresh, skip the soaking. After 10 minutes, drain and set aside.

Meanwhile prepare the sauce. In a small bowl, combine all the sauce ingredients and mix well.

Place the chicken in a bowl, add 3 tablespoons (45 ml) of the sauce and toss together. Set aside.

Coat a large, heavy, lidded skillet or wok with cooking oil and place it over medium-high heat. Add the chicken, onion, cabbage, rice cakes, sweet potato wedges and perilla leaves. Drizzle the rest of the sauce over the vegetables.

When you hear the loud sizzling sound, stir-fry the mixture to ensure all the ingredients are coated with the sauce, about 2 minutes. Drizzle the cola over the mixture, cover it and cook for 5 minutes over medium heat.

Remove the cover. Add the leek and toss together. Stir-fry until the rice cakes and vegetables are tender, 2 to 3 minutes. Sprinkle with the sesame seeds and serve hot.

**COOK'S TIP:** If you have room for more food after finishing the dakgalbi, try stir-frying some cooked rice with the sauce that remains in the skillet over high heat. Add a little bit of sesame oil, sesame seeds and crumbled roasted seasoned seaweed (page 142), and toss it all together. Eat immediately. It is fantastic!

# ANDONG-STYLE BRAISED CHICKEN WITH NOODLES

**(ANDONG JJIMDAK, 안동찜닭)**

## SERVES 4 TO 6

4 oz (115 g) Korean sweet potato noodles

1 (3-lb [1.4-kg]) chicken, cut into pieces, skin removed if possible

5 to 6 dried chiles

1 medium onion, sliced

2 to 3 medium carrots, peeled and cut into ½" (1.3-cm)-thick slices

10.6 oz (300 g) Yukon Gold potatoes, peeled and cut into ½" (1.3-cm)-thick slices

1 to 2 fresh green chiles, sliced

1 green onion, finely chopped, for garnish

2 tsp (5 g) toasted sesame seeds, for garnish

Cooked rice, for serving

### BROWN SUGAR SOY SAUCE

½ cup (120 ml) soy sauce

2 tbsp (30 ml) oyster sauce

1 cup (240 ml) water

¼ cup (56 g) dark brown sugar

¼ cup (60 ml) Korean oligo syrup or corn syrup

2 tsp (5 g) unsweetened cocoa powder

3 cloves garlic, minced

1 tsp pureed fresh ginger

1 tsp freshly ground black pepper

There are many ways to cook chicken in Korean cuisine. Here is one popular braised chicken dish that came from a city called Andong in the southeastern part of Korea. The chicken is simmered in flavored soy sauce with vegetables and sweet potato noodles, and it's slightly spicy. You will find a very unusual ingredient in this recipe. It is my secret that makes this chicken extra special—everyone who has tried it has told me that mine was the best jjimdak they've ever had. Now I am going to reveal my secret to you—but you'll have to look for it buried in the ingredients list. Slurping the chewy sweet potato noodles is often more enjoyable than the chicken itself to many people (including me), so don't skip the noodles. Make sure to drizzle the gravy over the rice. It is to die for!

Soak the sweet potato noodles in warm water for 20 minutes; set aside.

Bring a large pot of water to a boil over high heat. Add the chicken pieces and boil them for 3 minutes. Remove the chicken and discard the water. Place the chicken in a colander; set aside.

In a small bowl, mix together all the sauce ingredients. The cocoa powder won't mix in very well and that is okay.

Return the chicken to the empty pot and add the dried chiles. If you want to increase the spiciness, break a few of the dried chiles to release their seeds. Pour the sauce mixture over the chicken, cover it and cook for 10 minutes over medium heat, or until the chicken is mostly cooked.

Turn the chicken over, making sure to coat it evenly with the sauce. Add the onion and carrots to the pot; stir, re-cover it and cook for another 7 to 8 minutes over medium heat. Add the potatoes and cover it again, but leave an opening for the steam to escape this time. Cook until the vegetables are almost tender, 3 to 5 minutes.

Drain the water from the sweet potato noodles and add them to the pot along with the fresh green chile. Increase the heat to medium-high and continue to cook, uncovered, for another 3 to 5 minutes, tossing occasionally.

When the vegetables are tender and the noodles are soft yet chewy, remove it from the heat. Let the stew sit for 5 minutes, uncovered, to allow the chicken and the noodles to soak up the flavor. Transfer the chicken, vegetables and noodles to a large serving platter and drizzle with the gravy. Garnish with the green onion and sesame seeds. Serve hot with a little bit of rice.

# CHICKEN GINSENG SOUP
## SERVES 2

⅓ cup (65 g) uncooked sweet short-grain rice

1 (3-lb [1.4-kg]) chicken, or 2 Cornish hens

8 to 10 cloves garlic

4 to 5 dried jujubes

1 to 2 fresh ginseng, or 1 (2.4-oz [70-g]) packet samgyetang herb mix

7 to 8 cups (1.7 to 1.9 L) water

2 tbsp (12 g) chopped Asian leek or green onion

1 tsp kosher salt

½ tsp freshly ground black pepper

Cabbage kimchi (page 146) or radish kimchi (page 149), for serving

## COOK'S TIPS:

Although this soup calls for ginseng, you can also use a dried Korean herb mix packet that is prepared solely for making samgyetang. You can easily find it in Korean grocery stores.

Sweet short-grain rice (chapssal) is stickier and more glutinous than regular short-grain rice. It is whiter and more opaque than regular short-grain rice, which is more translucent.

For some reason, years ago someone decided that samgyetang was a good dish to beat the heat of the hot summer in Korea, so Koreans like to eat this boiling hot soup during the hottest season of the year. It is believed that the combination of chicken, ginseng and herbs will strengthen our resistance to the heat. Or it could simply be that you sweat so much while eating this boiling hot soup that you forget about how hot it is outside. To be authentic, use tiny spring chickens so that one whole chicken serves one person. You can use Cornish game hens, or use a young, whole chicken and share. The easiest way to cook samgyetang would be in a pressure cooker, but you can also prepare it on the stove (it just takes longer). You will love the fragrant, herb-infused broth.

Soak the sweet rice in cold water for 30 minutes and drain.

Cut off and discard the wing tips and the loose skin and fat near the tail. Remove any major fat around the chicken as well. Rinse the chicken thoroughly and stuff it with the rice and garlic, adjusting the amount depending on the size of the chicken you use, making sure to leave room for the rice to expand during cooking. Place 1 dried jujube to cover the cavity opening. With a knife, poke a hole, about ½ inch (1.3 cm) long, near the bone of 1 drumstick. Cross the chicken legs and put the other drumstick through the hole so the legs are crossed and secured, or simply cross the legs and tie them with string. This will help hold the stuffing in the cavity.

**To cook the chicken in an electric pressure cooker,** put the chicken in the pressure cooker, add the rest of the jujubes and the herbs and add enough of the water to barely cover the chicken. Cook the chicken for 20 minutes and let the steam vent naturally for 10 minutes. Turn the knob to quick release to let all the pressure out.

**To cook the chicken on the stovetop,** place the chicken, remaining jujubes and the herbs in a heavy-bottomed pot, and pour in enough of the water to barely cover the chicken. Bring it to a gentle boil first, then cover it and simmer over low heat for 40 minutes.

To serve, the chicken should be very tender and fall apart easily with a fork. Transfer the chicken to a large serving bowl and pour the hot broth over it. Sprinkle the leek on top. Mix together the salt and pepper in a small serving bowl. Present the chicken soup hot with the salt and pepper mixture on the side.

If you are enjoying the whole chicken by yourself, tear off a piece of chicken meat and dip it in the salt and pepper mixture to season as you eat. You also will need to season the broth with the salt and pepper mixture to taste. Don't forget to enjoy the rice inside the chicken. If sharing, tear all the meat off the chicken and put it back into the broth. Scoop the rice out of the chicken and add it to the soup as well. Divide the soup into individual bowls and season with the salt and pepper mixture. Enjoy the soup with cabbage kimchi or radish kimchi on the side.

## (DAKNANGCHAE, 닭냉채)

# KOREAN CHICKEN SALAD
## SERVES 6 TO 8

3 boneless, skinless chicken breast halves

8 oz (225 g) mung bean sprouts

Salt

1 small onion, thinly julienned

1 small red bell pepper, seeded and thinly julienned

1 small yellow pepper, seeded and thinly julienned

½ English cucumber, thinly julienned

¼ small red cabbage, shredded

1 sweet apple, thinly sliced

2 fresh perilla leaves, thinly julienned, for garnish (optional)

### MUSTARD DRESSING

2 tsp (10 g) prepared Korean mustard

1 tbsp (15 ml) soy sauce

¾ tsp salt

¼ cup (60 ml) fresh lemon juice

¼ cup (84 g) honey

2 tsp (10 ml) sesame oil

1 clove garlic, finely minced

2 tbsp (16 g) toasted sesame seeds, crushed

This elegant chicken salad is sure to please a crowd. It is often served in Korea as a main dish to guests during the hot summer season. Traditionally, poached chicken breast is used, but you can certainly use store-bought rotisserie chicken instead. Use any vegetables you like that are suitable for a salad. Korean mustard (yeongyeoja) is nose-tinglingly spicy and more mustardy than yellow mustard. It is easily found in Korean groceries but you can substitute whole-grain mustard if you can't find Korean mustard. Make sure all the ingredients are kept cold before you serve.

Poach the chicken breast in simmering water over low heat, about 20 minutes, until tender. Let the chicken cool a little and shred it to bite size. Cover it and chill in the refrigerator.

Bring a pot of water to a boil and blanch the mung bean sprouts with some salt for 10 seconds. Using a colander, drain and rinse with cold water. Chill in the refrigerator.

Meanwhile, prepare the dressing. In a small bowl, combine all the dressing ingredients and whisk well. Chill in the refrigerator.

On a large serving platter, arrange the salad ingredients in a pleasing pattern, placing the shredded chicken in the center and garnishing with the perilla leaves, if using.

To serve, divide the salad among individual serving dishes and drizzle with the dressing. Toss and serve immediately.

**(GOGALBI, 고갈비)**

2 fresh mackerels, cleaned and filleted

Cooking oil, for pan

Salt

Freshly ground black pepper, divided

½ lemon

2 tbsp (33 g) Korean chili paste

2 tbsp (13 g) Korean chili flakes

1 tbsp (15 ml) soy sauce

1 tbsp (21 g) honey

1 tbsp (15 ml) Korean plum extract (optional)

2 cloves garlic, finely minced

1 tsp pureed fresh ginger

1 tbsp (15 ml) sesame oil

2 tsp (5 g) toasted sesame seeds

1 green onion, chopped, for garnish

Cooked rice, for serving

# BROILED SPICY MACKEREL
## SERVES 4

Gogalbi is a well-known fish dish from Pusan, a city on Korea's southern coast. Traditionally, fresh mackerel fillets are grilled over charcoal, brushed with a spicy sauce then finished again over the grill to set the sauce. However, you don't need to fire up your charcoal grill. Here is an easy version you can make in an oven that is every bit as delicious as the traditional gogalbi. Fresh mackerel is readily available in any Korean store these days. Remember to ask your grocer to clean and fillet it for you.

Pat the mackerel fillets with a paper towel to remove any water on the surface. Preheat the oven to 425°F (220°C) and line the grill part of your broiler pan with a piece of foil on the bottom to catch any drippings—this will make cleanup much easier. Grease the foil with cooking oil, then place the fillets on the pan and sprinkle them very lightly with salt and black pepper. Squeeze the lemon over the fillets.

Bake the fish for 10 to 12 minutes, depending on the thickness, or until they're firm and cooked thoroughly.

While the fish cooks, in a small bowl, combine the chili paste, chili flakes, soy sauce, honey, plum extract (if using), garlic, ginger, sesame oil, sesame seeds and a pinch of black pepper and mix well; set aside.

When the fish is firm and thoroughly cooked, remove the pan from the oven. Adjust the oven rack to 6 inches (15 cm) below the heat source and turn on the broiler to high. Spread the spicy sauce evenly on top of each fillet. Return the pan to the oven and broil for 1 to 2 minutes. The sauce will start to bubble quickly. Watch carefully so you do not burn the sauce. Garnish with green onion and serve warm with rice.

**COOK'S TIP:** If you can't find fresh mackerel, you can use frozen salted mackerel. Get a pan that is long enough to fit the fillets into, and before putting in the fish, pour in enough cold water to cover the fillets. Whisk in 2 to 3 tablespoons (15 to 23 g) of all-purpose flour into the water until it becomes milky. Then, place the frozen fillets in the flour water and let them soak for 15 to 20 minutes. The flour water will not only defrost the fillets, but also get rid of the saltiness and reduce the fish smell during the cooking. I can't explain the science behind it, but that's what many Koreans do and it always works!

**( H A E M U L J J I M ,  해물찜 )**

# SPICY SEAFOOD & BEAN SPROUTS
## SERVES 4 TO 6

6 large dried anchovies, deveined, head removed

3 cups (720 ml) water

1 lb (455 g) soybean sprouts, cleaned

2 tbsp (30 ml) Korean soy sauce for soup

2 tbsp (30 ml) sweet rice wine (mirin)

¼ cup (25 g) Korean chili flakes

2 tbsp (33 g) Korean chili paste

2 tsp (9 g) sugar

1 tsp pureed fresh ginger

1 tbsp (10 g) finely minced garlic

½ tsp freshly ground black pepper

3 lb (1.4 kg) assorted seafood (crab, mussels, squid, shrimp), cleaned and cut

¼ cup (32 g) potato starch

¼ cup (60 ml) water

2 tsp (10 ml) sesame oil (optional)

1 tbsp (8 g) sesame seeds, for garnish

1 green onion, finely chopped, for garnish

**If you are a seafood lover, this is the dish of your dreams. Various kinds of seafood are tossed in a spicy sauce—you'll be licking the tastiness from your fingers. The addition of soybean sprouts offers a deliciously crunchy texture. I like to take the time to remove the yellow heads and tail parts of the soybean sprouts, but you don't have to. As long as your seafood is precleaned and ready to cook, the entire dish can be ready to serve within 15 minutes.**

In a large, lidded pan or wok, combine the dried anchovies and water and add the bean sprouts on top; do not mix. Cover it and bring to a boil. Lower the heat to low and let it simmer for 3 to 4 minutes. Using kitchen tongs, transfer the bean sprouts to a strainer; set aside. Pick out the anchovies and discard them; reserve the stock in the pan.

In a small bowl, combine the soy sauce, rice wine, chili flakes, chili paste, sugar, ginger, garlic, black pepper and ¼ cup (60 ml) of the reserved stock to create a chili sauce; mix well and set aside.

Bring the remaining stock to a boil again over medium-high heat. Add the crab pieces first, cover it and cook for 2 to 3 minutes. Add the rest of the seafood and cover it with the soybean sprouts. Drizzle the chili sauce over the top and cover it again. Cook over medium-high heat for 3 to 4 minutes.

In another small bowl, combine the potato starch with the water and mix well.

Lift the lid and, using tongs or a spatula, stir the seafood and soybean sprouts in the chili sauce until it's mixed thoroughly. Add about two-thirds of the starch mixture to the pan and continue to cook over medium-high heat to thicken. Add more of the starch mixture until the sauce is your desired consistency.

Remove the pan from the heat. Drizzle the sesame oil, if using, on the top and sprinkle with the sesame seeds and green onion. Serve immediately.

**COOK'S TIP:** Handling seafood often leaves an odor on the cutting board or on kitchen utensils. The best way to get rid of it is to use brown sugar. Rub your cutting board or other kitchen utensil with brown sugar and rinse it thoroughly. Scrub your hands with brown sugar as well. It exfoliates your skin, leaving your hands soft and odorless.

**(SSAMBAP, 쌈밥)**

# RICE & FISH LETTUCE WRAPS
## SERVES 4

2 tsp (10 ml) cooking oil

½ small onion, finely chopped

1 tbsp (10 g) minced garlic

½ (2-oz [56-g]) zucchini, finely chopped

½ cup (120 ml) water

2 tbsp (33 g) Korean fermented soybean paste

1 tbsp (16 g) Korean chili paste

1 tbsp (15 ml) soy sauce

½ tsp sugar

1 (14-oz [400-g]) can mackerel pike, drained, 3 tbsp (45 ml) liquid reserved

1 to 2 green chiles, sliced

1 green onion, chopped

Freshly ground black pepper

Assorted lettuce, such as Bibb, romaine, or green leaf, for serving

Cooked rice, for serving

Steamed cabbage and/or pumpkin leaves, for serving

Perilla leaves, for serving

*Ssam* means "to wrap" (with lettuce) and *bap* means "rice," so *ssambap* is literally a rice wrap. It is a rustic Korean food, popular during the hot summer season. Typically, it is served with mixed-grain rice, topped with a delicious fish topping sauce and wrapped in a variety of lettuce and leaves. Canned mackerel pike (kkongchi) comes in very handy to prepare the sauce, and you can find it in any Korean grocery store. It is inexpensive and has very little fish odor. Since the fish is already cooked to be very tender, you can actually eat the bones with the meat. Serve it with a variety of lettuce. Steamed cabbage leaves and pumpkin leaves are also great to serve together. Ssambap is my kids' absolute favorite Korean food, and you never know, it might become your favorite too.

In a small pot, heat the oil over medium-high heat. Add the onion and garlic and cook until soft, 2 to 3 minutes. Add the zucchini and cook for another minute.

Add the water and, using a wooden spoon, smear the soybean and chili pastes into the pot until they're mixed into the water. Add the soy sauce, sugar, canned fish and its reserved liquid to the pot, breaking the fish into large chunks with the spoon. Add the green chile and bring the sauce to a boil, then simmer it for 7 to 8 minutes over medium-low heat, or until the sauce thickens. Remove it from the heat, and add the green onion, black pepper and stir; the sauce will thicken further as it cools.

Arrange the assorted lettuce leaves on a large serving platter or in a basket. Put the fish mixture in a small bowl.

To serve, put a spoonful of rice on a lettuce, cabbage, pumpkin or perilla leaf, or a combination of 2 to 3 leaves, and top with a tablespoon (15 ml) of the sauce. Close the lettuce to cover the rice and topping and put it into your mouth. Savor this little piece of heaven!

**COOK'S TIP:** If your lettuce seems lifeless, bring it to life quickly by rinsing it under warm water for 1 minute. It will come back to life much quicker than by soaking it in cold water. The ideal temperature of the water is about 120°F (50°C)—about right for most people to take a shower in. In fact, you should wash most vegetables and fruits in warm, not cold, water. The vegetables absorb the water a lot faster in warm water and it makes them crisper. It also cleans off pesticides or other impure substances that might dwell on the surface, and it increases the freshness and sweetness of the vegetables and fruits.

# ONE-DISH
## WONDERS

**WE ALL NEED** meals in our culinary repertoire that are simple to prepare, yet delicious. Korean cuisine provides many tasty alternatives that are simple and healthy for our modern, hectic lifestyles.

First, let's learn a few Korean words that you've probably seen on the menu at your local Korean restaurant. The word for "cooked rice" in Korean is bap. Throw on a couple of syllables on the front and you've got bibimbap, which is rice with at least two or more toppings and a separate sauce that you must mix together to serve. Dupbap is usually a rice bowl that has seasoned meat or another main dish on top of rice that you eat as is. Bokkeumbap is literally "fried rice." And lastly, kimbap is rice with other various ingredients rolled in a sheet of seaweed.

In this chapter are nine easy-to-prepare and delicious Korean rice bowl dishes that you can serve to your family and friends without the hassle of cooking an entire multicourse meal. These authentic Korean rice bowls are quick enough to enjoy on busy weeknights and scrumptious enough that you'll want to have them on the weekends, too. They are simple, enjoyable, and most of all, good-for-you meals that you'll feel satisfied about serving to your loved ones.

# STEAK & AVOCADO RICE BOWL

## SERVES 4

## FRUITY SOY SAUCE DRESSING

6 tbsp (90 ml) soy sauce

3 tbsp (45 ml) sea kelp stock or water (see Cook's Tip)

3 cloves garlic, minced

1½ tbsp (20 g) sugar

¼ Asian pear or sweet apple, seeded and thinly sliced

Freshly ground black pepper

1½ tbsp (23 ml) sesame oil

1½ tbsp (12 g) toasted sesame seeds

1½ lb (680 g) beef skirt steak or hanger steak, at room temperature

Salt

Freshly ground black pepper

1 tbsp (15 ml) cooking oil

4 servings cooked white or brown rice

2 ripe avocados, peeled, pitted and cubed

2 oz (56 g) baby arugula (optional)

3 to 4 pink radishes, thinly sliced, for garnish (optional)

Why not add a simple modern twist to the traditional bibimbap? This healthy salad-like rice bowl is adorned with tender, juicy beef, soft avocado chunks and crisp baby arugula, then drizzled with a fruity soy sauce dressing. You will be surprised because it is pleasing not just to the eye, but also to your taste buds. I recommend using skirt steak or hanger steak for their deep beefy flavors, but any of your favorite cuts of beef will work fine.

To prepare the dressing, in a small saucepan, combine the soy sauce, sea kelp stock, garlic, sugar and pear slices. Bring it to a boil over medium-high heat. Turn off the heat and let it cool for 5 minutes. Discard the pear slices and add pepper to taste. Add the sesame oil and sesame seeds; stir well. Set aside.

Heat a grill pan or skillet over medium-high heat. Season the steak with salt and pepper to your liking. Add the oil to the hot pan, sear the steak on both sides and cook to your desired doneness, 3 to 5 minutes per side for medium doneness. Remove the steak from the pan and let it rest for 5 minutes. Slice the steak thinly against the grain.

Place each serving of rice in an individual shallow serving bowl; top with the steak, avocado cubes, arugula and radish slices, if using. Drizzle with the dressing, 1 to 2 tablespoons (15 to 30 ml) per bowl. Serve immediately.

To eat the traditional bibimbap, you must mix all the ingredients together just before you begin to eat.

**COOK'S TIP:** Sea kelp stock is very easy and quick to make. Combine 1 cup (240 ml) of water with a small piece of dried sea kelp (dashima) in a small saucepan and bring it to a gentle simmer, 3 to 5 minutes. Turn off the heat and discard the kelp. There you go—you've got sea kelp stock! Keep any leftover stock in the fridge for 1 week or freeze it for later use.

## (SAESSAK BIBIMBAP, 새싹비빔밥)

# SALAD SPROUTS RICE BOWL WITH MEAT SAUCE
## SERVES 8

### MEAT SAUCE
½ large Korean or Asian pear, peeled, seeded and diced

¼ large onion, diced

2 cloves garlic

1 tbsp (15 ml) cooking oil

4 oz (115 g) ground beef

6 tbsp (99 g) Korean chili paste

2 tbsp (42 g) honey

1 tbsp (15 ml) sesame oil

1 tbsp (8 g) toasted sesame seeds


8 cups (1.4 kg) cooked rice, for serving

About 6 oz (170 g) total of assorted sprouts (e.g., pea, radish, alfalfa or other edible sprouts)

3 oz (85 g) young spring greens

1 English cucumber, cut into thin matchsticks

¼ small red cabbage, shredded

8 red young radishes, cut into thin matchsticks

Edible flowers, for garnish (e.g., pansies, lavender, violets or sage blossoms) (optional)

This salad sprout rice bowl is not just another pretty face—it is a delectable bibimbap to serve family and friends. One good thing is that you don't need to cook the main ingredients, since they are sprouts and spring greens. The MVP award for this dish, however, goes to the meat sauce called yak gochujang. This mildly spicy and sweet beef sauce is the perfect match for this rice bowl. You can make the simple sauce well ahead of time. Once the sauce is ready, this naturally beautiful dish can be put together in a snap. Use a variety of edible sprouts (and flowers) and unleash your inner artist. You'll create a healthy rice bowl that just might be too beautiful to eat!

For the meat sauce, in a blender, puree the pear, onion and garlic together until smooth. Set aside.

Heat the cooking oil in a skillet over medium-high heat. Add the ground beef and cook until done, making sure there are no big clumps of meat.

Add the pear puree, chili paste and honey; mix well and bring it to a gentle boil. Lower the heat to medium-low and cook, stirring occasionally, until the sauce thickens to a thin paste, 4 to 5 minutes.

Add the sesame oil and sesame seeds and stir well. Remove it from the heat and let the sauce cool. It will thicken more as it cools. Store the meat sauce in the fridge for up to 3 weeks. It makes a wonderful topping for plain cooked rice.

To assemble the rice bowls, put 1 serving of the rice in a small rice bowl and press down gently to mold the rice into the shape of the bowl. Turn over the rice bowl in the center of a large individual serving bowl. Arrange the sprouts and salad vegetables around the rice. Adorn with edible flowers, if using. Serve with the meat sauce, 1 to 2 tablespoons (15 to 30 g) per serving, on top or in a separate small bowl on the side.

When ready to eat, use a pair of chopsticks to toss the rice, salad and sauce together. Don't try to coat every salad and rice grain with the sauce completely. A brief tossing is all you need.

**COOK'S TIP:** Traditionally, most bibimbap is served with a light soup on the side. Try this with Kale Soy Soup (page 109). The earthy flavor from the soybean paste, kale and tofu will complement the rice bowl nicely.

## (MOO GOOLBAP, 무굴밥)

# OYSTER-RADISH RICE BOWL
## SERVES 4

1¼ cups (243 g) uncooked short-grain white rice

1 (6" [15-cm]) piece dried sea kelp

1¼ cups (300 ml) water

16 oz (455 g) jarred fresh-shucked oysters or frozen oysters

10½ oz (300 g) Korean radish

### SOY CHILI SAUCE

¼ cup (60 ml) soy sauce

1 tbsp (15 ml) water

1 tbsp (6 g) Korean chili flakes

½ tsp sugar

1 clove garlic, finely minced

1 green onion, finely chopped

1 fresh green chile, thinly sliced (optional)

1 fresh red chile, thinly sliced (optional)

1 tbsp (15 ml) sesame oil

1 tbsp (8 g) toasted sesame seeds

**When fresh oysters are in season at wintertime, try this healthy, simple rice bowl dish that you can make in one pot. Korean radishes are also in season throughout the winter, and their sweet and mellow flavor will go very well with the oysters. You can use shucked fresh oysters in a jar or even frozen oysters to keep it simple. The sauce is essential since it will be the main seasoning for the dish.**

Rinse the rice in water 3 or 4 times, in a large bowl. Pour in fresh water to fill the bowl. Soak the rice for 30 minutes.

Meanwhile, soak the dried sea kelp in the 1¼ cups (300 ml) of water for 30 minutes. When done, discard the sea kelp and reserve the water.

Drain the liquid from the oysters if using jarred and rinse them gently with water. Set aside.

Peel the radish. Cut the radish into ¼-inch (6-mm) slices and julienne them into ¼-inch (6-mm)-thick matchsticks.

Drain the rice and place it in a large pot. Spread the radish on top of the rice and pour the reserved sea kelp water over the top. Cover the pot with a lid and cook over medium-high heat until it just begins to boil. Immediately lower the heat to low and let it simmer for 15 minutes.

Open the lid and gently stir the rice and radish with a fork. Add the oysters to the pot and cover it with a lid again; simmer for another 5 minutes. Turn off the heat and let the pot rest, covered, on the stove for another 4 to 5 minutes. The steam inside the pot will finish cooking the ingredients; so don't let it out too soon.

Meanwhile, prepare the sauce. In a small bowl, combine all the sauce ingredients; set aside.

When the rice mixture is ready, gently toss it with a rice paddle or spoon so that the rice, radish and oysters are evenly mixed.

To serve, scoop your desired amount into a serving bowl and serve with the sauce. Mix the sauce with the rice just before eating. You can add more sauce, if needed.

## BEEF & CUCUMBER RICE BOWL

**SERVES 4**

1 lb (455 g) NY strip or sirloin steak

1½ tbsp (23 ml) Korean soy sauce for soup

2 tbsp (30 ml) sweet rice wine (mirin) (optional)

2 tsp (9 g) sugar

3 cloves garlic, minced

2 tsp (10 ml) sesame oil

A few pinches of freshly ground black pepper

16 oz (455 g) cucumbers

1 tsp kosher salt

2 tbsp (30 ml) cooking oil, divided

1 red chile, sliced thinly (optional)

2 to 3 green onions, chopped

2 tsp (5 g) toasted sesame seeds

4 cups (696 g) cooked rice, for serving

Fresh cucumbers are tasty, but stir-fried cucumbers are divine. They become irresistibly crunchy and mellow without the bitterness you can find in raw cucumbers. When you have abundant summer cucumbers on hand, try this healthy, low-calorie meal. It is super quick and simple to make. I recommend using Kirby, Korean or English cucumbers for this recipe.

Slice the beef very thinly across the grain and place it in a bowl. Add the Korean soy sauce for soup, rice wine (if using), sugar, garlic, sesame oil and black pepper; toss and massage the seasoning into the beef. Set aside to marinate for 10 minutes.

Cut the cucumbers in half lengthwise. Using a spoon, scoop out and discard the seeds, then thinly slice the cucumbers diagonally. Place the slices in a bowl and sprinkle with the salt; toss well and set aside for 10 minutes. Squeeze the cucumber slices to remove the extra moisture; set aside.

In a large skillet, heat 1 tablespoon (15 ml) of the oil over medium heat. Add the cucumber slices and stir-fry them for 2 minutes. Transfer the cucumbers to a plate.

In the same skillet, heat the remaining oil over high heat. Add the beef and red chile, if using, and stir-fry until the beef is browned. Return the cucumber slices to the skillet along with the green onions. Stir-fry for 30 seconds. Turn off the heat, sprinkle with the sesame seeds and toss well. Serve with the rice.

**(GAJI DUPBAP, 가지덮밥)**

# EGGPLANT & CRISPY MINCED PORK RICE BOWL

## SERVES 4

### CRISPY MINCED PORK

1 lb (455 g) minced pork

2 tbsp (30 ml) sweet rice wine (mirin)

1 tbsp (13 g) sugar

2 cloves garlic, finely minced

1 tsp pureed fresh ginger

½ tsp freshly ground black pepper

1 tbsp (15 ml) cooking oil

3 tbsp (45 ml) soy sauce

2 tsp (10 ml) sesame oil

2 to 3 green onions, sliced

1 fresh red chile, seeded and sliced (optional)

3 Asian eggplants (about 27 oz [760 g])

1½ tbsp (23 ml) Korean soy sauce for soup

1 tsp sesame oil

1 tbsp (8 g) toasted sesame seeds

4 cups (696 g) cooked rice, for serving

Eggplant is usually a love-it-or-hate-it kind of vegetable. If your family has not been fond of eggplant, try it again in this Korean-style rice bowl. The crisp minced pork tossed with tender steamed eggplant is a delicious and healthy one-bowl meal that just might change their perception of eggplant. Look for thin and slender Asian eggplants. Their skin is much softer and less bitter. If you can't find them, peel off the skin of the thick Western eggplant.

In a bowl, combine the pork, rice wine, sugar, garlic, ginger and black pepper; mix well with your hands.

Heat a skillet until very hot over medium-high heat. Drizzle the cooking oil into the skillet and add the pork; stir-fry until the pork is no longer pink and the moisture has evaporated, 3 to 4 minutes. Drizzle in the soy sauce and sesame oil and continue to stir-fry until the pork feels dry and crisp, 2 to 3 minutes. Remove it from the heat and set the skillet aside.

In a large bowl, combine the green onions and red chile, if using.

Heat a steamer over boiling water. Cut each eggplant into 4 sections and cut each section into 4 to 6 segments lengthwise. Put the eggplant slices into the hot steamer and steam for 2 to 3 minutes, covered.

Transfer the hot, steamed eggplant immediately on top of the green onions and chile. Let it sit for 2 minutes. The heat of the eggplant will soften the green onions and chile. Add the Korean soy sauce for soup and the sesame oil and toss gently to coat.

Add the crispy pork to the eggplant mixture and sprinkle with the sesame seeds; gently toss together. Serve over the rice.

**COOK'S TIP:** Crispy minced pork is very versatile to use in other dishes. You can make a quesadilla with it and some meltable cheese and a tortilla. You can also stir-fry it with fresh rice cakes, sprinkle it over salad or simply serve over rice. I often double the recipe and cook the pork until crisp. Once it has cooled, I divide it into small, resealable plastic freezer bags and freeze it for later use.

## (BEOSUT GEUNDAEBAP, 버섯근대밥)

# MUSHROOM-SWISS CHARD RICE BOWL
### SERVES 4

### RICE MIXTURE

1½ cups (293 g) uncooked white or brown rice

1 tbsp (15 ml) cooking oil

½ large onion, chopped

1 bunch Swiss chard (about 8 oz [225 g]), sliced

¼ tsp salt

12 oz (340 g) total assorted mushrooms of your choice, sliced or torn if needed

### SEA KELP STOCK

1 (6" [15-cm]) piece dried sea kelp

3 cups (720 ml) water

### TOFU SOYBEAN SAUCE

¼ (4-oz [115-g]) package soft tofu

1 tbsp (15 ml) cooking oil

¼ large onion

2 cloves garlic

3 tbsp (49 g) Korean fermented soybean paste

1 tsp Korean chili paste

1 green onion, finely chopped

Kimchi, for serving

**COOK'S TIP:** You can make this rice bowl much quicker in an electric pressure cooker. If using white rice, there is no need to soak it in water. If using brown rice, soak it for at least 30 minutes. Sauté the onion, Swiss chard and rice first, and then add the mushrooms and only 1½ cups (360 ml) of sea kelp stock. Cook on the rice setting for 12 minutes. Allow 10 minutes of natural steam release after the cooking cycle is finished, and then turn the vent knob for a quick steam release.

If you love mushrooms, this rice bowl is right for you. Any mushrooms will work for this recipe, but I suggest using varieties of Asian mushrooms, such as shiitake, oyster and enoki mushrooms. Their chewy textures and fragrances are pleasant to enjoy in a rice bowl and they go very well with Swiss chard. I like to make this rice bowl with brown rice, which requires a longer soaking time if cooked on a stovetop. You can also use an electric pressure cooker to reduce your preparation time. The rustic flavor of the tofu soybean sauce perfectly matches this rice bowl, giving you a true taste of Korea's countryside cuisine.

Wash and rinse the rice and soak it in water (30 minutes for white rice, 2 hours or up to overnight for brown rice). Drain the rice and set aside.

For the stock, in a medium saucepan, combine the sea kelp and the 3 cups (720 ml) of fresh water and simmer for 5 minutes over low heat. Discard the sea kelp and set the stock aside. You should have at least 2¾ cups (660 ml) of stock.

To cook the rice mixture, in a large, heavy-bottomed pot, heat the oil over medium-high heat. Add the onion and cook until soft. Add the Swiss chard and salt and sauté until soft. Add the rice and stir to mix.

Pour 2 cups (480 ml) of reserved sea kelp stock into the rice mixture; bring it to a boil. Add the mushrooms and stir. Cover it and lower the heat to low; simmer for 20 minutes to allow the rice to cook. Turn off the heat and let it sit for 5 minutes.

Meanwhile, prepare the tofu soybean sauce. Smash the soft tofu with the side of your knife until you get small crumbs. Set aside.

In a small saucepan, heat the oil over medium-high heat. Add the onion and garlic and cook until soft. Add the soybean paste and chili paste and mix well. Add the crushed tofu and ¾ cup (180 ml) of the remaining sea kelp stock. Bring it to a boil, then lower the heat to medium-low to thicken the sauce, about 5 minutes. Add the green onion and stir.

Fluff the rice mixture in the pot, making sure all the ingredients are evenly mixed. Serve the rice mixture in individual serving bowls topped with the tofu soybean paste sauce, 2 to 3 tablespoons (30 to 45 g) per serving. When ready to eat, mix the rice with the sauce and enjoy it warm, with kimchi on the side (of course).

**(DAKGOGI DUPBAP, 닭고기덮밥)**

# SPICY CHICKEN & ZUCCHINI RICE BOWL
## SERVES 4

1½ lb (680 g) boneless, skinless chicken thighs

1 tbsp (15 ml) sweet rice wine (mirin)

1 tsp pureed fresh ginger

1 tsp kosher salt, plus more to sauté

¼ tsp freshly ground black pepper, plus more to sauté

2 to 3 tbsp (30 to 45 ml) cooking oil, divided

1 medium onion, sliced

2 zucchini, sliced

½ cup (64 ml) cornstarch or all-purpose flour

4 cups (696 g) cooked rice, for serving

### CREAMY CHILI SAUCE

1 tbsp (16 g) Korean chili paste

1 to 2 tbsp (6 to 13 g) Korean chili flakes

1 tbsp (14 g) mayonnaise

1 tbsp (15 ml) soy sauce

2 tbsp (42 g) honey

2 tbsp (30 ml) sweet rice wine (mirin)

1 tbsp (10 g) minced garlic

¼ cup (60 ml) water

1 tbsp (15 ml) sesame oil

1 tbsp (8 g) toasted sesame seeds

Busy weeknight? If you have 30 minutes, you can prepare this quick and easy chicken rice bowl. You will love the creamy sweet and spicy chili sauce that goes with the chicken and sautéed vegetables. Don't skip the mayonnaise in the sauce—a little goes a long way. It helps thicken the sauce and makes the sauce velvety; you won't even taste the mayo. The sauce is great to mix with plain rice, or use over other types of meat. I used zucchini and onion to accompany the chicken in this scrumptious rice bowl, but pretty much any variety of vegetable would work.

In a bowl, toss together the chicken, rice wine, ginger, salt and black pepper. Set aside for 10 minutes.

For the sauce, in a small skillet, mix together all the sauce ingredients, except the sesame oil and sesame seeds. Bring it to a boil and cook for 30 seconds. Remove it from the heat and add the sesame oil and sesame seeds. Stir well and set aside. The sauce will thicken more as it cools.

In a large skillet, heat 1 tablespoon (15 ml) of the cooking oil over medium heat. Add the onion and zucchini slices and sauté until they're tender but crisp, about 3 minutes. Season lightly with salt and black pepper. Remove them from the skillet and set aside.

Add more oil to the skillet and heat it. Lightly coat the chicken thighs with the cornstarch. Add the chicken to the skillet and cook for 3 to 4 minutes, or until golden brown. Turn the thighs to the other side and continue to cook for another 3 minutes, or until the chicken is fully cooked, adding more oil as needed. Slice the chicken thighs into large bite-size strips.

To serve, place the rice in individual serving bowls and top with chicken strips and vegetables. Drizzle with the sauce. Serve warm.

# KIMCHI PORK FRIED RICE
## SERVES 3 OR 4

**(KIMCHI BOKKUMBAP, 김치볶음밥)**

1 tbsp (15 ml) cooking oil

1 tbsp (14 g) unsalted butter

⅔ cup (66 g) finely chopped Asian leek or green onion

8 oz (225 g) minced pork or diced ham

1½ cups (375 g) sour cabbage kimchi (page 146), finely chopped

1 tsp sugar

1 tbsp (15 ml) soy sauce

3 tbsp (45 ml) kimchi liquid

3 cups (510 g) cooked white rice

Salt (optional)

1 tbsp (15 ml) sesame oil

1 tbsp (8 g) toasted sesame seeds

3 or 4 large eggs

1 to 2 sheets roasted seasoned seaweed, torn (optional) (page 142)

**If you have too much sour kimchi and perhaps even leftover rice, this recipe comes to the rescue. There are hundreds of recipes for kimchi fried rice and here I add mine to the list. Pork or pork products (ham and bacon) are the best companions for kimchi, but minced chicken, turkey or shrimp are good with it, too. Although it may sound untraditional, using a little bit of butter makes this kimchi fried rice more tasty, in my humble opinion.**

In a large skillet, heat the oil and butter over medium-high heat. Add the leek and stir-fry for 30 seconds. Add the pork and cook until the pork is no longer pink, 2 to 3 minutes.

Add the kimchi and sugar; stir-fry for 3 minutes. Drizzle the soy sauce into the skillet and let it evaporate, 30 seconds. Add the kimchi liquid and cook for 1 more minute.

Lower the heat to medium-low, add the rice and toss together to incorporate well, breaking up any big lumps of rice. Season the fried rice with salt, if needed. Remove the skillet from the heat, add the sesame oil and sesame seeds and toss well.

Meanwhile, in another skillet, fry the eggs to your desired doneness (typically sunny-side up).

Place the kimchi fried rice in individual serving bowls and top with a fried egg. Sprinkle with the roasted seaweed, if using. Serve hot.

# OODLES OF
## NOODLES

**IMAGINE YOURSELF** enjoying a bowl of noodles that is so scrumptious that you forget about all the slurping sounds you make. According to Korean table manners, it is not polite to make a slurping noise when you eat, but doing so is an unmistakable sign that the noodles are really yummy. The sound will (secretly) be music to the cook's ears.

The noodle dishes in this chapter are so good that you will find it hard not to slurp. Some are slathered in delicious sauce, and some are in a soup form that are comforting for either cold or hot days.

Koreans like to use various kinds of noodles. Sweet potato noodles (dangmyun) are unique to Korean cuisine. The noodles becomes translucent when cooked and offer a chewy and delightful texture. Different varieties of wheat noodles and rice noodles are also widely used in Korean noodle dishes.

Whatever type of noodles you choose, these simple recipes are sure to please all your noodle lovers.

# EASY FESTIVE SWEET POTATO NOODLES WITH VEGETABLES

## SERVES 6

1 (8-oz [230-g]) bundle sweet potato noodles

2 tbsp (30 ml) cooking oil

8 oz (225 g) beef striploin or sirloin, sliced into thin strips

3 cloves garlic, minced

1 medium onion, sliced

1 large carrot, thinly julienned

5 oz (140 g) shiitake mushrooms, stems removed, sliced

5 tbsp (75 ml) soy sauce

2½ tbsp (33 g) sugar

½ cup (120 ml) water, plus more as needed

8 oz (225 g) spinach

1 tbsp (15 ml) sesame oil

1 tbsp (8 g) toasted sesame seeds

½ tsp freshly ground black pepper

Japchae, made with sweet potato noodles called dangmyun, is the most popular Korean noodle dish that everyone loves. Making japchae in the traditional way, however, can be daunting because each ingredient requires many steps to prepare. So, you love the world-famous Korean noodles, but don't want all the complicated steps? This recipe comes to the rescue! You will be able to prepare these delicious festive Korean noodles with ease anytime and every time. If you have patience to soak the sweet potato noodles for 30 minutes, you can cook the entire dish within the next 10 minutes. Seriously!

Soak the sweet potato noodles in warm water for 30 minutes. Drain and rinse them several times. Cut the noodles with a pair of kitchen shears, if desired. Set aside.

In a very large skillet or wok, heat the oil over medium-high heat. Add the beef and garlic and stir-fry for 1 minute. Add the onion, carrot and mushrooms and continue to stir-fry for another 2 minutes.

Add the soy sauce and sugar and toss well. Add the sweet potato noodles and the fresh water and toss everything very well. Lower the heat to medium and cover; continue to cook for 5 minutes.

Remove the lid and add the spinach on top. If there is no liquid on the bottom of the skillet, add a little more water. Cover again and cook for another 2 to 3 minutes.

When the spinach leaves are all wilted, toss everything to mix well. Remove the skillet from the heat and add the sesame oil, sesame seeds and pepper; mix well. Serve warm.

**COOK'S TIP:** Leftover japchae should be stored in the fridge. Using a microwave to reheat the japchae is, unfortunately, not ideal since the texture of the noodles won't be the same. I recommend using the stovetop method. Heat a little oil in a skillet over medium heat, add the japchae and stir-fry until heated through, 2 to 3 minutes. You can enjoy them again as if they were just made for you.

## (JAPCHAE SALAD, 잡채새우샐러드)

### SERVES 4

5½ oz (150 g) Korean sweet potato noodles

¾ lb (340 g) shrimp, deveined

½ English cucumber

¼ large red onion, thinly sliced

1 carrot, thinly julienned

½ red bell pepper, thinly julienned

### CHILI VINAIGRETTE

3 tbsp (45 ml) soy sauce

2 tsp (10 ml) grapeseed oil

1½ tsp to 1 tbsp (3 to 6 g) Korean chili flakes

2 tbsp (30 ml) rice vinegar

2 tbsp (26 g) sugar

1 tbsp (8 g) toasted sesame seeds

¼ tsp freshly ground black pepper

Fresh cilantro, for garnish (optional)

Korean sweet potato noodles, dangmyun, are very versatile. You can use them to create many delicious dishes, including salads. Here is an easy salad you can try with whatever vegetables you have on hand. The noodles will stay chewy for many hours without going soggy, so you can make this salad ahead of time. I used red bell pepper and cucumber, but blanched spinach, asparagus, green beans or mung bean sprouts would also work very well. The simple Korean chili vinaigrette is just the right dressing to bind them all together with a hint of a spicy kick. Try this salad with poached shrimps. Shredded or grilled chicken, minced beef or pork or even some seared tofu would also be lovely with this salad.

Bring a pot of water to a boil. Cook the sweet potato noodles according to the package directions, 5 to 6 minutes. Drain the noodles in a colander and rinse them with cold water several times. Cut the noodles with kitchen shears if desired; set aside.

In a medium saucepan, poach the shrimp in simmering water over medium heat for 2 to 3 minutes, or until they are fully cooked. Drain the shrimp and set aside.

Cut the cucumber in half lengthwise and scrape out and discard the seeds with a spoon. Slice the cucumber thinly.

In a large bowl, combine the noodles, shrimp, cucumber slices, red onion, carrot and bell pepper.

In a small bowl, mix together the soy sauce, oil, chili flakes, vinegar, sugar, sesame seeds and black pepper. Whisk until the sugar dissolves. Pour the dressing over the salad and toss everything together. Garnish with cilantro, if using. Serve immediately or chill for up to 4 hours.

## (JJAJANGMYUN, 짜장면)

## SERVES 4

2 tbsp (30 ml) cooking oil

2 green onions, chopped

8 oz (225 g) pork loin, chopped

1 medium onion, finely chopped

2 cloves garlic, finely minced

1 tbsp (15 ml) soy sauce

¼ small green cabbage, finely chopped

1 small zucchini, finely chopped

¼ cup (66 g) preroasted black bean paste (see Cook's Tip)

2¾ cups (660 ml) water, divided

1 tsp sugar

2 tbsp (16 g) cornstarch

2¼ lb (1 kg) fresh thick wheat noodles

Originally from China, jjajangmyun has long been a favorite noodle dish at Chinese-style Korean restaurants. The thick wheat noodles covered with mellow black bean sauce are sure to please young and old alike. It is easy to make and enjoy this classic noodle dish. Look for preroasted Korean-style black bean paste in a jar, called chunjang. Having preroasted chunjang will save an extra step getting the sauce ready. Fresh wheat noodles are easy to find in the refrigerator section of any Asian grocer, but you can also use dried wheat noodles.

In a wok or deep skillet, heat the oil over high heat. Add the green onions and stir-fry for 30 seconds. Add the pork, onion and garlic and stir-fry until the pork is fully cooked and the onion is soft, 2 to 3 minutes.

Drizzle in the soy sauce. Add the cabbage and continue to stir-fry for another minute. Add the zucchini and stir-fry for another 30 seconds.

Add the black bean paste and mix everything to coat well. Pour in 2½ cups (600 ml) of the water and add the sugar; mix well. Bring the sauce to a gentle boil. Lower the heat to medium-low and let it simmer for 4 to 5 minutes, or until all the vegetables are tender.

In a small bowl, whisk together the cornstarch and remaining ¼ cup (60 ml) of water. Add the mixture to the sauce and stir. Cook until the sauce thickens, 1 to 2 minutes.

Meanwhile, in a large pot, cook the wheat noodles according to the package directions. Drain the noodles in a colander. Transfer the noodles to individual serving bowls and ladle the sauce over the top. Serve immediately.

**COOK'S TIPS:** If you'd rather use plain, unroasted Korean black bean paste, you will need to perform the roasting yourself first to get rid of the paste's bitterness.

Heat ¼ cup (60 ml) of oil in a wok over medium heat. Add the ¼ cup (66 g) of bean paste and 1 teaspoon of sugar; stir-fry for about 2 minutes. Be careful not to burn the paste. The oil and the paste won't mix, but you need the oil to keep the paste from scorching and sticking to the pan. Using a slotted spoon, scoop up the paste from the oil and place it in a bowl. Discard the oil.

## (JJAMPPONG, 짬뽕)

SPICY NOODLE SOUP
WITH SEAFOOD

# SPICY NOODLE SOUP WITH SEAFOOD

### SERVES 4

3 tbsp (45 ml) cooking oil

1 Asian leek or 2 green onions, finely chopped

¼ cup (25 g) Korean chili flakes

12 oz (340 g) pork shoulder or butt, thinly sliced

½ large onion, sliced

½ green cabbage (14 oz [400 g]), thinly sliced

1 carrot, thinly sliced

8 cups (1.9 L) low-sodium chicken stock

3 lb (1.4 kg) assorted seafood (squid, mussels and shrimp), cleaned

2 tbsp (30 ml) Korean soy sauce for soup, plus more to taste

Salt

Freshly ground black pepper

1.6 lb (750 g) thick wheat noodles

This is another Korean/Chinese-style classic noodle soup that is very popular in Korea. *Jjamppong* literally translates to "mixed everything." Classic jjamppong should have pork mingled with a variety of seafood and served with noodles all together in one bowl. It is important to infuse the chili flakes in oil over low heat prior to adding the meat and vegetables. This noodle soup is easy to make at home and very quick to put together if your seafood is already well cleaned. I recommend using fresh seafood for the best flavor, but frozen seafood will work, too.

In a large pot or wok, heat the oil over medium-low heat, then sauté the leek for 1 minute. Add the chili flakes and stir-fry for 30 to 60 seconds.

Increase the heat to medium or medium-high. Add the pork and stir-fry until cooked, 2 to 3 minutes. Add the onion, cabbage and carrot and stir-fry for 2 minutes.

Pour in the chicken stock and stir. Bring it to a boil. Lower the heat to medium-low, cover and simmer for 3 to 5 minutes.

When the vegetables are tender, add the seafood and cook for 2 to 3 minutes, or until the seafood is fully cooked; do not overcook. Season with 2 tablespoons (30 ml) of Korean soy sauce for soup and add more to taste. Add salt and black pepper to taste.

Meanwhile, in a large pot cook the noodles according to the package directions. Drain the noodles and distribute them among individual soup bowls. Pour the soup and the seafood over the noodles. Serve immediately.

**COOK'S TIPS:** To clean the mussels, pull off the brown coarse hair from the side. Rub the mussels against each other under running water.

To devein the shrimp, peel off the shell and cut a slit on the back of the shrimp.

To clean the squid, separate the tentacles from the tube by pulling apart with a slight twisting motion. Insert your finger into the tube to remove the cuttlebone (cartilage). Tear off the bony beak from the base of the tentacles and discard it. Cut the squid tube in half lengthwise and score it with a knife on the inside. Slice it into ½-inch (1.3-cm)-thick pieces. The scoring on the squid will make a pleasing visual pattern when cooked.

## (DAKSUJEBI, 닭수제비)

## SERVES 4

2¼ lb (1 kg) boned chicken pieces

10 oz (280 g) Korean radish or daikon radish, diced

1 large onion, quartered

8 large dried anchovies, deveined, head removed

1 (6" [15-cm]) piece dried sea kelp

5 cloves garlic

2 tsp (9 g) Korean salted shrimp

8 cups (1.9 L) water

1 large carrot, sliced

1 zucchini, diced

2 green onions, chopped

### POTATO DUMPLINGS

2 cups (250 g) all-purpose flour

1 cup (225 g) plain cooked mashed potatoes

1 large egg, beaten

½ tsp salt

½ cup (120 ml) water

2 tsp (10 ml) cooking oil

### SOY CHILI SAUCE

¼ cup (60 ml) Korean soy sauce for soup

1 to 2 tbsp (6 to 13 g) Korean chili flakes

2 cloves garlic, finely minced

1 fresh chile, minced (optional)

1 tbsp (15 ml) sesame oil

1 green onion, finely chopped

Kimchi, for serving

Sujebi are simple flour dumplings that are torn into pieces by hand and cooked in a type of stew. Korean mothers often wrap the sujebi dough in plastic bags and give it to children to play with. The kids have fun squishing the dough, but their mothers know they are actually kneading the dough while they are getting the rest of the ingredients ready. Some kids often go to such lengths as to put the wrapped dough on the floor and hop on it with their bare feet as they watch TV. Don't worry—Korean mothers have the wisdom to wrap the dough multiple times! This comforting stew, simmered with chicken and vegetables together, makes a wonderful warm stew for a cold day. Don't worry about the long ingredient list. This dish is simple and quick to make once the stock is ready.

In a large soup pot, combine the chicken, radish, onion, anchovies, sea kelp, garlic and salted shrimp. Pour in the water, cover and bring it to a gentle boil over high heat. Lower the heat to low and simmer for 30 minutes. Remove the chicken from the pot and set it aside to cool. Strain the stock, saving only the liquid, discarding the vegetables, anchovies and shrimp. Shred the chicken meat and set it aside.

Meanwhile, prepare the dumplings. In a medium bowl, combine the flour, mashed potatoes, egg and salt. Add the water and oil and mix well with a fork. Knead the dough for 2 to 3 minutes. The dough should be thick and slightly stiff, but pliable. Form the dough into a ball and cover it with a clean kitchen towel. If you have time, let the dough chill for 30 minutes, to provide a chewier texture.

In a small bowl, mix together all the sauce ingredients. Set aside.

In the large soup pot, bring the reserved stock to a boil over medium heat. Add the carrot and the shredded chicken. When the carrot is slightly tender, 2 to 3 minutes, add the zucchini.

Take a chunk of the dough and, working quickly, tear it into bite-size pieces with your hands and add it to the pot as you go. Repeat with the remaining dough. You don't need to make uniformly shaped dumplings. When the dumplings float to the top and the vegetables are tender, the stew is ready to serve. Sprinkle the chopped green onion into the pot and stir.

Since the stock is not fully seasoned, you will need to serve with the soy chili sauce. To serve, add a tablespoon (15 ml) of the sauce to each individual serving of the stew and stir gently. Add more sauce, if needed. Serve hot with kimchi on the side.

# CLAM NOODLE SOUP

## (BASIRAK KALGUKSU, 바지락칼국수)

### SERVES 4

2¼ lb (1 kg) fresh littleneck clams

2 tbsp (36 g) salt

2 tbsp (30 ml) vinegar

10 cups (2.4 L) water

7 to 8 large dried anchovies, deveined, head removed

1 (6" [15-cm]) piece dried sea kelp

8 oz (225 g) Korean radish, diced

1 carrot, thinly sliced

1 zucchini, thinly sliced

1 medium russet potato, peeled and sliced

1.6 lb (750 g) fresh thick wheat noodles

## SOY CHILI SAUCE

¼ cup (60 ml) soy sauce

2 tbsp (13 g) Korean chili flakes

1 fresh chile, minced (optional)

1 green onion, finely chopped

2 cloves garlic, finely minced

1 tbsp (15 ml) sesame oil

Freshly ground black pepper, to taste

Cabbage kimchi (page 146), for serving

Here is a simple noodle soup for clam lovers. Look for fresh littleneck clams. They are easy to handle and perfect for a noodle soup. As for the noodles, you can purchase Korean-style thick wheat noodles in the refrigerator section of any Korean grocery. Alternatively, you can try fettuccine or even rice noodles. The soup broth is unseasoned, so make sure to serve this dish with the topping sauce—and cabbage kimchi on the side is a must!

Prepare the clams in advance, preferably the night before. Rub the fresh clams with the salt and rinse them well under running water. Place the clams in a large bowl with plenty of water. Add the vinegar and cover the bowl with a dark cloth or plastic bag. Store it in the fridge until ready to use.

To prepare the soup, in a large pot, combine the fresh water, dried anchovies, sea kelp and radish. Bring it to a boil and remove and discard the sea kelp. Lower the heat to low and simmer for 10 minutes. Discard the anchovies and radish and reserve the stock. Set aside.

In a small bowl, mix together all the sauce ingredients, adding black pepper to taste; set aside.

Take the clams from the fridge and discard the water. Rinse them again and drain in a colander.

Bring the anchovy stock to a gentle boil. Lower the heat to medium-low. Add the carrot and cook until tender, 2 to 3 minutes. Add the zucchini, potato and clams and continue to simmer until the clams are cooked, 2 to 3 minutes (their shells will open). Discard any clams that fail to open.

Meanwhile, in a separate pot, cook the wheat noodles according to the package directions, 4 to 5 minutes. Drain the noodles in a colander.

Divide the noodles among individual serving bowls and ladle the soup, including the clams and vegetables, over the noodles. To serve, top each serving of the soup with about 1 to 2 tablespoons (15 to 30 ml) of the soy chili sauce and mix it well in the soup. Serve with cabbage kimchi on the side.

## (OJINGUH CHOMUHCIM, 오징어초무침)

2 squid (about 1 lb [455 g] total), tentacles separated, head and innards removed

¼ small green cabbage, thinly sliced

1 cucumber, cut in half lengthwise and thinly sliced

1 small carrot, thinly sliced into matchsticks

¼ large onion, thinly sliced

½ Korean pear, peeled and thinly sliced (optional)

3 tbsp (49 ml) Korean chili paste

2 tbsp (13 g) Korean chili flakes

2 tbsp (30 ml) rice vinegar

1 tbsp (10 g) finely minced garlic

1½ tbsp (20 g) sugar

2 tbsp (30 ml) Korean plum extract

1 tbsp (8 g) toasted sesame seeds

½ lb (250 g) thin wheat vermicelli noodles

# COLD VERMICELLI WITH SPICY SQUID SALAD

## SERVES 4

Spicy squid salad over cold thin vermicelli is a popular summer noodle dish. Tender, chewy squid that has been properly cooked, along with the crunchy vegetables tossed in a tangy spice sauce will bring anyone's lost appetite back. You can also enjoy the squid salad with rice instead of noodles. Make sure to not to overcook the squid, otherwise it will get rubbery. The Korean plum extract or syrup (mashil-cheong) will enhance the flavor of the sauce. If you can't find it, you can substitute lemon juice and oligo syrup.

Bring a pot of water to a boil. Slice open the squid tubes vertically and then score the inside flesh of the tube diagonally. Cut them to your desired size. Cut the tentacles into 2 to 4 pieces. Add the squid pieces and tentacles to the boiling water and cook for 1 to 2 minutes. Drain and set them aside to cool.

When the squid has cooled, in a large bowl, combine the squid, cabbage, cucumber, carrot, onion and Korean pear, if using.

In a small bowl, mix together the chili paste, chili flakes, vinegar, garlic, sugar, plum extract and sesame seeds. Pour the sauce over the squid mixture. Toss everything together with your hands to incorporate the sauce evenly.

Meanwhile, cook the noodles according to the package directions, 4 to 5 minutes. Drain the noodles in a colander and rinse them under cold running water several times until they are completely cooled.

Take a portion of the noodle strands with 1 hand and wrap them around 2 or 3 fingers of the other hand to make a nest. Continue until you have made all the noodles into nests, Place the noodle nests and squid salad on a serving platter.

To serve, put a noodle nest and some salad in an individual serving bowl. Each guest should toss the noodles and salad together with a pair of chopsticks before eating.

**COOK'S TIP:** If you don't have Korean plum extract, substitute with a mixture of 1 tablespoon (15 ml) each of fresh lemon juice and Korean oligo syrup or corn syrup.

## NOODLES WITH SEASONED SOY SAUCE

### (MATGANJANG BIBIMGUKSU, 맛간장비빔국수)

**SERVES 4**

Matganjang is a seasoned soy sauce that is widely used in Korean home cooking. It is very easy to make and can be used as a replacement for plain soy sauce to boost the flavor of many dishes. The sauce will stay fresh up to one month in the fridge. I recommend doubling or tripling the recipe for the seasoned soy sauce so you'll have it on hand for many other Korean dishes. Here is a simple noodle dish that is flavored with this delicious sauce. Topped with caramelized onion, cucumber and egg, this is an easy and inexpensive way to feed a crowd.

### SEASONED SOY SAUCE

½ cup (120 ml) soy sauce

½ cup (120 ml) water

4 tbsp (60 ml) sweet rice wine (mirin)

2 tbsp (30 ml) rice syrup or corn syrup

3 dried shiitake mushrooms

1 small onion, unpeeled and quartered

1 (6" [15-cm]) piece dried sea kelp

3 fresh whole green chiles

### NOODLES

2 tbsp (30 ml) cooking oil, divided

1 large onion, thinly sliced

1 tsp sugar

½ tsp salt, plus more to taste

1 English cucumber, sliced into thin strips

3 large eggs, beaten

½ lb (250 g) thin wheat vermicelli noodles

1 tbsp (15 ml) sesame oil

½ tsp freshly ground black pepper

1 tbsp (8 g) sesame seeds

In a small pot, stir together all the seasoned soy sauce ingredients and bring it to a gentle boil over medium-high heat. Cover, lower the heat to low and let it simmer for 20 minutes. Strain the sauce through a fine sieve to collect the sauce. Discard the vegetables. Set the sauce aside.

For the noodles, in a skillet, heat 1 tablespoon (15 ml) of the oil over medium heat and add the onion. Cook the onion, stirring occasionally, for 6 to 8 minutes, or until it turns golden brown. Lower the heat to medium-low. Add the sugar and a pinch of salt and continue to cook as the onion caramelizes, 3 to 4 minutes, or until it is deep brown. Remove it from the skillet and set it aside.

Meanwhile, in a bowl, toss the cucumber with ½ teaspoon of salt and let it sit for 5 minutes. Squeeze the excess moisture from the cucumber. In a clean skillet, heat 1½ teaspoons (8 ml) of the remaining oil and stir-fry the cucumber for 1 to 2 minutes. Remove the cucumber from the skillet and set it aside.

In a nonstick skillet, heat the remaining 1½ teaspoons (8 ml) of oil over medium-low heat. Pour in the beaten eggs and let it cook for 1 minute. Turn it to the other side and cook for another 30 seconds, or until it's fully cooked. Turn out the cooked egg onto a cutting board, roll it up and slice it very thinly into thin strips; set aside.

Cook the noodles according to the package directions. Drain in a strainer and rinse them with cold water several times. Drain the noodles well.

Place the noodles in a large bowl and add half of the seasoned soy sauce, all of the sesame oil and black pepper, plus two-thirds each of the caramelized onion, cucumber and egg. Using your hand or kitchen tongs, toss everything together. You can add more sauce as necessary. Transfer the noodle mixture to a serving platter and top with the remaining onion, cucumber and egg. Sprinkle with the sesame seeds and serve immediately.

# HEART-WARMING
## SOUPS & STEWS

**SOUPS AND STEWS** are a must-have in homestyle Korean meals. Taking their place beside the main dish, rice and many side dishes, soups and stews are essential to round out any Korean table.

From a light soup to accompany the main meat dish to a hearty stew that becomes a meal of its own, Korean soups and stews have an important place in the Korean feast. In fact, mastering these dishes is key to succeeding in Korean cooking.

Many Korean soups and stews require a soup stock called yuksu. The most common yuksu is made with dried anchovies (myulchi) and/or dried sea kelp (dashima). Fortunately, this stock is very quick and easy to make, requiring only a few minutes of simmering. Some varieties of yuksu only use sea kelp to flavor the soup, such as in Restaurant-Style Beef Soybean Paste Stew (page 113) and Spicy Squash & Pork Stew (page 118). Others, such as Kale Soy Soup (page 109) and Soft Tofu Stew (page 117), use both dried anchovies and sea kelp. Throughout this chapter, you will find simple instructions on how to make these stocks. The stock rarely stands out in the finished dish, but it adds an undertone of rich flavor that completes the soup. If you want to enjoy authentic Korean soups and stews, stocking up on dried anchovies and sea kelp is a must.

## (DAEPA YUKGAEJANG, 대파육개장)

# SPICY BEEF & ASIAN LEEK SOUP
## SERVES 4 TO 6

1 lb (455 g) beef brisket, flank or eye round

1 onion, quartered

8 oz (225 g) Korean radish or daikon radish, diced

8 cloves garlic, divided

8 whole peppercorns (optional)

8 cups (1.9 L) water

10 oz (280 g) Asian leek

2 tbsp (30 ml) grapeseed or sunflower oil

1 to 2 tbsp (6 to 13 g) Korean chili flakes

1 tsp Korean chili paste

5 oz (140 g) oyster or shiitake mushrooms, sliced (optional)

1 tbsp (15 ml) Korean soy sauce for soup

1 tbsp (15 ml) Korean tuna sauce or anchovy sauce

½ tsp freshly ground black pepper

2 large eggs lightly beaten (optional)

Cooked rice, for serving

Kimchi, for serving

Asian leeks look like gigantic green onions. You can find them in many Asian grocery stores. They turn very tender and chewy in soups and stews. This recipe is a simplified version of the classic Korean spicy soup called yukgaejang that features shredded beef and a variety of Korean vegetables. With this recipe, you will enjoy the equally good-tasting yukgaejang minus all the complicated prep work. The spiciness is adjustable, based on how much chili flakes you want to add. After all, this simple yukgaejang is not overly spicy. It is a soul-comforting, flavorful beef soup for cold days (although I love it on warm days, too). I like to include mushrooms for added flavor, but you can leave them out, if you wish.

In a large pot, combine the beef, onion, radish, 5 of the garlic cloves, the peppercorns (if using) and the water. Bring it to a very gentle boil and simmer for 45 minutes over low heat. Let the stock cool for 10 minutes, then strain it through a mesh strainer to collect the broth. Reserve the beef and 5 to 6 cups (1.2 to 1.4 L) of the broth. Discard the vegetables. Shred the beef and set it aside.

Meanwhile, mince the remaining 3 garlic cloves. Slice the leeks in half lengthwise and cut them into pieces 2 inches (5 cm) long (both the white and up to half of the green part). Set aside.

In a soup pot, heat the oil over medium-low heat until warm. Add the chili flakes and stir for 1 minute. Be careful not to burn the chili flakes; adjust the heat level, if needed. Add the chili paste and incorporate it with the chili flakes. Add the shredded beef and coat it with the chili mixture.

Increase the heat to medium. Pour in about 5 cups (1.2 L) of the broth and add the mushrooms. Bring it to a gentle boil.

Add the leek and minced garlic and continue to simmer for 3 minutes over medium-low heat. Add more broth, if needed; it should just cover both the meat and leeks. Add the Korean soy sauce for soup and tuna sauce to season the soup. Adjust the seasoning according to your taste. Add the black pepper and stir, then cook until the leeks are tender.

If you want to add eggs to the soup, just before serving, drizzle the beaten eggs over the soup and stir briefly, just a couple of times, so that you can keep a few chunks of egg. Cover it with a lid and let it simmer for another minute. Serve hot with rice and kimchi on the side.

## (KALE DOENJANGGOOK, 케일된장국)

### ANCHOVY SEA KELP STOCK (MYULCHI YUKSU)

4 cups (960 ml) rice starch water (see Cook's Tip on page 113) or plain water

5 to 6 large dried anchovies, deveined, head removed

2 (6" [15-cm]) pieces dried sea kelp

### SOUP

3 tbsp (49 g) Korean fermented soybean paste

4 oz (115 g) baby kale

½ (8-oz [225-g]) package soft tofu, diced

2 cloves garlic, minced

1½ tsp (3 g) Korean chili flakes (optional)

2 tsp (10 ml) Korean anchovy sauce, or a pinch of salt

1 fresh red chile, sliced (optional)

1 green onion, chopped

Cooked rice, for serving

# KALE SOY SOUP
### SERVES 4

Deep green vegetables are perfect to use in this Korean-style simple soup made with soybean paste. This comforting soup is nourishing, flavorful and not too heavy. I used baby kale for this recipe but regular kale is fine as well. Experience has shown that curly leaf kale tastes better than the flat kind with this soup. Turnip greens and Swiss chard are also wonderful to use in place of kale.

In a soup pot, combine the rice starch water, dried anchovies and sea kelp and bring it to a boil over medium-high heat. Turn off the heat, remove the sea kelp and let the stock sit for 5 minutes. Remove the anchovies, using a slotted spoon, and discard.

Return the soup pot to medium heat. Dissolve the soybean paste into the stock by smearing the paste against the side or bottom of the pot, using the back of a wooden spoon, and then stirring. Add the kale and bring it to a gentle boil. Add the tofu and garlic. Lower the heat to low and simmer for 5 to 7 minutes, or until the kale is tender.

Add the chili flakes, if using, and season with anchovy sauce or salt. Finally, sprinkle in the red chile (if using) and green onion. Serve hot with rice.

## (GAJAMI MIYUKGOOK, 가자미미역국)

0.8 oz (22 g) dried seaweed

1¼ lb (560 g) whole white fish, such as flounder (whole or cut into pieces), scaled and gutted

6 cups (1.4 L) water

1 tsp sesame oil

1 tsp cooking oil

1 tbsp (15 ml) Korean soy sauce for soup

1 tbsp (15 ml) Korean anchovy sauce or tuna sauce

Salt (optional)

1 tbsp (10 g) finely minced garlic

Cooked rice, for serving

Kimchi, for serving

**COOK'S TIPS:** Look for smaller whole flounder or other flatfish, such as dab fish. I promise that this soup won't leave any fish odor behind. Even though your fish guy cleaned the fish for you, your fish still might have some scales. Using a knife, starting from the tail toward the head, scrape the fish to remove any remaining scales on every corner of the fish. Rinse it very well before cooking.

The dried seaweed (miyuk) used in this recipe is like twigs, not to be confused with seaweed that comes in flat sheets (gim). It is light as a feather and you only need a very small amount, but when soaked in water, it will expand to more than quadruple in volume in just 10 minutes.

# FISH & SEAWEED SOUP
## SERVES 4

Did you know that seaweed soup is a traditional birth day soup in Korea? Most Korean mothers eat seaweed soup for a few days right after they deliver a baby. Seaweed is rich in iodine, which increases hormonal metabolism and helps mothers produce more breast milk for nursing. Whereas those in the northern part of Korea tend to eat their seaweed soup with beef, those in the south like to use fish or other seafood in their seaweed soup.

This is my mother's signature soup recipe that I adore. A whole flatfish is simmered to produce the delicious stock. The result is a silky smooth and mellow seaweed soup with tender white fish. The recipe itself is very simple. My mother always added the garlic as the final step. I love the garlicky kick it brings.

In a large bowl filled with water, soak the dried seaweed for 10 minutes.

Place your fish in a pot and add the 6 cups (1.4 L) of fresh water. Bring it to a gentle boil over medium-high heat, then simmer for 15 minutes over low heat. Using a spoon, scoop out any foam forming on the surface of the broth. Remove the fish from the broth and let it cool. Reserve the broth.

Meanwhile, remove the seaweed from the soaking water. Drain it and squeeze out the excess moisture. Chop to your desired size.

In a soup pot, heat the sesame and cooking oils over medium heat. Add the chopped seaweed and stir-fry for 1 minute. Add about ½ cup (120 ml) of the reserved fish broth and continue to stir for another 1 minute. Add the rest of the fish broth and bring the soup to a gentle boil. Cover, lower the heat to low and simmer for 20 minutes.

When the fish is cool enough to handle, using a spoon or knife, scoop out the flesh from the bones. Make sure to remove all the small bones near the side fins of the fish. The flesh should come off very easily. Discard the bones. Put the fish meat back into the soup and simmer for 3 to 4 minutes.

Season with the soy sauce for soup and the anchovy sauce. If needed, add salt according to your taste. Then, add the garlic and remove the pot from the heat. Serve the soup hot with rice and kimchi on the side.

## (SOGOGI DOENJANG JJIGAE, 소고기된장찌개)

1¾ cups (420 ml) rice starch water (see Cook's Tip)

1 (3" [7-cm]) piece dried sea kelp

4 oz (115 g) beef stew meat with some fat or marbling, thinly sliced

¼ medium onion, sliced

1 small Yukon Gold potato (about 2 oz [55 g]), peeled and finely diced

2 tbsp (33 g) Korean fermented soybean paste

1 tbsp (16 g) Korean seasoned soybean paste

1 tsp Korean chili flakes

¼ cup (18 g) finely chopped shiitake or cremini mushrooms

4 oz (115 g) tofu, diced

½ zucchini, diced

1 clove garlic, finely minced

1 fresh green chile, sliced

Cooked rice, for serving

# RESTAURANT-STYLE BEEF SOYBEAN PASTE STEW
## SERVES 2 TO 3

Some of the best-tasting doenjang jjigae varieties are served in Korean barbecue restaurants. The flavorful soybean paste stew with a hint of spicy kick is often the grand finale of a heavy meal of barbecue. Many restaurants use a unique ingredient that you don't find in the home-style doenjang jjigae: well-marbled beef (or another cut with some fat attached), which I use for this stew. The fat brings out the flavor. Also, I recommend saving the water that you used to wash the rice. Using the saved rice starch water (ssal-tte-mul) for stew is a common practice of Korean home cooks, especially for doenjang jjiage. It will help thicken the stew and bind the paste to the broth. Please do not simmer this stew for too long, to preserve the deep flavor of the soybean paste.

In a pot, combine the rice starch water, sea kelp, beef, onion and potato. Bring it to a boil over medium-high heat and cook for 3 to 4 minutes. Discard the sea kelp.

Using the back of a wooden spoon, 1 spoonful at a time, smear the soybean pastes into the mixture and mix well. Sprinkle in the chili flakes and stir. Add the mushrooms, tofu and zucchini; continue to boil for another minute, or until the vegetables are just soft. Adjust the heat to medium or medium-low, so the stew doesn't boil too rapidly.

Add the garlic and green chile to the stew, heat it through and then remove the pot from the heat. Serve hot with rice.

**COOK'S TIP:** To make rice starch water, rinse uncooked rice with cold water and drain and discard the first rinsed water. Swirl the rice with your hand rapidly for 30 seconds. Pour the desired amount of water you need for the recipe over the rice and swirl again. You will see the water turn milky as some starch emerges from the rice. Pour the milky water into a bowl to collect. Continue to finish washing the rice as usual.

## KIMCHI PORK STEW

**(DOEJI KIMCHI JJIGAE, 돼지김치찌개)**

### SERVES 4 TO 6

1 tbsp (15 ml) cooking oil

10½ oz (320 g) pork shoulder or pork belly

½ medium onion, sliced

17.5 oz (500 g) sour cabbage kimchi (page 146), sliced (about 2 cups)

3 cups (720 ml) chicken stock

¼ cup (60 ml) kimchi liquid

1 tbsp (6 g) Korean chili flakes (optional)

1 sheet flat fish cake, diced

½ (6-oz [225-g]) package, soft tofu, diced

2 cloves garlic, minced

1 tbsp (15 ml) Korean soy sauce for soup

½ Asian leek or 1 green onion, sliced

Cooked rice, for serving

If your cabbage kimchi becomes too sour to eat as is, make a delicious stew with it. Overly fermented kimchi simmered with pork will make your taste buds come alive. Fatty pork cuts, such as pork shoulder or pork belly, plus chunks of tofu and a few pieces of fish cake make this stew rich to the taste and very comforting. You can leave out the fish cake, but it does add another layer of flavor and I highly recommend including it if you can. All you need is a bowl of rice to serve with this comforting stew.

In a heavy-bottomed soup pot, heat the oil over medium-high heat. Add the pork and onion and cook for 2 to 3 minutes. Add the kimchi and cook for another 1 to 2 minutes.

Add the chicken stock, kimchi liquid and chili flakes, if using, and stir. Cover and bring it to a gentle boil, then lower the heat to low and simmer for 20 minutes.

Add the fish cake, tofu and garlic to the stew and continue to simmer for another 10 minutes. Season the stew with Korean soy sauce for soup. Taste and adjust the seasoning to your liking. Add the leek and heat through. Serve hot with a bowl of rice.

## SOFT TOFU STEW

(SUNDUBU JJIGAE, 순두부찌개)

**SERVES 2**

### ANCHOVY SEA KELP STOCK (MYULCHI YUKSU)

2 cups (480 ml) water

4 large dried anchovies, deveined, head removed

1 (6" [15-cm]) piece dried sea kelp

2 tsp (10 ml) sunflower or grapeseed oil

2 tsp (10 ml) wild sesame or sesame oil

1 tbsp (6 g) Korean chili flakes

1½ tsp (8 g) Korean chili paste

¼ medium onion, chopped

8 oz (225 g) minced pork or beef

11 oz (312 g) extra-soft tofu

3 shiitake mushrooms, chopped

1 fresh chile, chopped

1 tsp Korean salted shrimp

2 to 3 tsp (10 to 15 ml) Korean soy sauce for soup

1 large egg (optional)

1 green onion, chopped

Cooked rice, for serving

Silky soft tofu in a flavorful spicy broth . . . if you are a Korean stew lover, then don't miss this comforting stew. This recipe contains my secret for making the best-tasting sundubu jjigae. The redness of the broth will remain vibrant until you finish the entire stew. Don't be scared by the color; it is not as spicy as it looks. Some people add seafood to this stew, but I like mine without, so that the tofu gets all the credit. Double or triple the recipe and make it in a bigger pot to serve a crowd. They will salute the chef!

For the stock, in a small pot, combine the water, anchovies (see Cook's Tip) and sea kelp and bring to a boil. Remove the sea kelp, lower the heat to low and simmer for 3 to 4 minutes. Discard the anchovies. Set aside.

In a medium pot, heat the sunflower and wild sesame oils over medium-low heat. Add the chili flakes and chili paste and stir until they are softened and fragrant, about 1 minute. Be careful not to burn the chili flakes; lower the heat, if needed.

Add the onion and cook for 1 minute. Increase the heat to medium, add the pork and stir until it is fully cooked, 1 to 2 minutes.

Pour 1 cup (240 ml) of the anchovy stock into the pot. Add the soft tofu, breaking it into big chunks with a spoon. Add the mushrooms. Bring the stew to a gentle boil and cook for 2 minutes.

Add the fresh chile and season the stew with salted shrimp and Korean soy sauce for soup. Adjust the seasoning according to your taste. Simmer for another 1 minute.

If you like, you can add an egg into the stew. Remove the pot from the heat. The remaining heat in the pot will cook the egg. Add the chopped green onion. To serve, gently break the egg yolk and stir a little. Serve immediately with rice and other side dishes of your choice.

**COOK'S TIP:** Dried shiitake mushrooms are handy to stock in your pantry for Korean stews. If you prefer not to use anchovy stock, use shiitake mushroom stock instead. Soak 3 dried mushrooms in hot water until they are fully rehydrated, 30 to 60 minutes. Reserve the soaking water to replace the anchovy stock.

# (AEHOBAK JJIGAE, 애호박찌개)

# SPICY SQUASH & PORK STEW
## SERVES 4

1 tbsp (15 ml) cooking oil

1½ tsp (8 ml) wild sesame or sesame oil

1 to 2 tbsp (6 to 13 g) Korean chili flakes

¾ lb (340 g) pork shoulder or butt, thinly sliced

1 small onion, thinly sliced

3 cups (720 ml) water

1 (4" [10-cm]) piece dried sea kelp

2 tbsp (33 g) Korean chili paste

1½ lb (680 g) squash or zucchini, sliced

2 cloves garlic, minced

1 tbsp (13 g) Korean salted shrimp, finely minced

1 Asian leek or 3 green onions, diced

2 tbsp (30 ml) Korean soy sauce

Cooked rice, for serving

This delicious spicy soup is famous in Korea's Jeolla province. The mellowness of the Korean squash pairs well with pork in a spicy broth made with chili oil and chili paste. Although it might look devilishly red, it is not overly spicy. You can always adjust the heat level for your liking. Use another kind of yellow squash or zucchini if you can't find Korean squash.

In a soup pot, heat the cooking and wild sesame oils over medium-low heat until slightly hot. Add the chili flakes and stir for 30 seconds, being careful not to burn the chili. Add the pork and cook for 2 to 3 minutes. Add the onion and continue to cook for another 1 to 2 minutes.

Pour the water into the pot and add the dried sea kelp. Increase the heat to high and bring it to a boil. Remove the sea kelp and discard. Lower the heat to low and simmer for 3 minutes.

Add the chili paste and stir well. Add the squash, garlic, salted shrimp and leek and simmer for 2 to 3 more minutes, or until the squash is soft and tender. Add the Korean soy sauce. Taste and adjust the seasoning according to your taste. Serve hot with rice.

# A BUNCH OF
# BANCHAN

**BANCHAN** is the word for "side dishes" in Korean. The best part of Korean cuisine to many people is the impressive array of attractive, colorful side dishes that accompany most Korean meals. No other country's cuisine offers such a variety of side dishes included in one single meal.

Although it can require a lot of work for Korean home cooks to prepare a different selection of banchan for every meal, the good news is that many of these side dishes can be made ahead of time and can be stored in the fridge. Some last a few days; others can last a few weeks. Don't tell your guests that you didn't actually prepare a dozen different side dishes all in one day!

The world-famous kimchi falls into the category of a side dish, but it is so integral to Korean cuisine that it also occupies its own very own category. Learn all about kimchi in the following chapter. Most Korean sides are made with different types of vegetables, meats and legumes.

Here you will find side dish recipes that are popular in Korean house-holds but are hard to find in your local Korean restaurants. These banchan recipes provide easy-to-make, delicious and healthy accompaniments to your Korean main course.

## PANFRIED TOFU WITH SOY CHILI SAUCE

**(DUBU BUCHIM, 두부부침)**

### SERVES 2 TO 4

1 (16-oz [455-g]) package firm tofu

Salt

1 tbsp (15 ml) cooking oil

1 tsp wild sesame or sesame oil

1 fresh red chile, chopped (optional)

### SOY CHILI SAUCE

2 tbsp (30 ml) soy sauce

1 tbsp (6 g) Korean chili flakes

2 tsp (10 ml) sesame oil

1 clove garlic, minced

1 green onion, chopped, plus more for serving

2 tsp (5 g) toasted sesame seeds

With a crisp texture on the outside and a soft chewy inside, panfried tofu with Korean chili sauce makes an appetizing side dish. In fact, it can even become a light meal served with a bowl of rice. Make sure to use firm tofu, not extra-firm. Mixing two different oils when frying adds more fragrance to the bland tofu. This is a quick, simple and super delicious way of enjoying tofu the Korean way.

Cut the tofu into 7 to 8 slices, about ½ inch (12 mm) thick. Lay the tofu slices flat on a cutting board and lightly sprinkle them with pinches of salt.

In a nonstick skillet, heat the cooking and wild sesame oils over medium heat. Press each tofu slice firmly between two paper towels to remove moisture from the surface, replacing the paper towels as they become saturated.

Place the tofu slices on the heated skillet. Sear them on one side until they're golden brown, 3 to 5 minutes. Turn the tofu slices to the other side and continue to sear for another 3 minutes. If you prefer a crispier texture on the outside, cook them longer. Adjust the heat so that it doesn't burn the tofu.

Meanwhile, prepare the sauce. In a small bowl, combine all the sauce ingredients and mix well.

Arrange the tofu slices on a serving dish and drizzle with the sauce. Garnish with chopped fresh chile (if using) and green onion. Serve warm or at room temperature.

**COOK'S TIP:** For perfect tofu, use a non-stick or well seasoned cast-iron skillet (I used my carbon steel skillet). The trick is to not flip the tofu too often. Flipping once is enough so that the surface of the tofu slices carmelizes.

## PANFRIED POTATO WITH VEGETABLES

### (GAMJA BOKKEUM, 감자볶음)

### SERVES 4

12 oz (340 g) Yukon Gold potato

¼ tsp salt, plus more to taste

½ medium carrot, peeled

½ green bell pepper, seeded

1 tbsp (15 ml) cooking oil

½ small onion, thinly sliced

2 cloves garlic, finely minced

Ground white pepper

1 tbsp (8 g) toasted sesame seeds

This is the Korean way of making a type of hash browns tossed with vegetables. It is a very simple dish to make, but you need to know some tips to keep the texture of the potato right. You want it soft and chewy, but not so soft that it falls apart. If you can slice a potato into thin matchsticks with your knife, you are well on your way toward becoming a master of Korean dishes. Use Yukon Gold potatoes or other buttery gold potatoes for this recipe. Don't be shy with the sesame seeds— we could all stand to have a little more nuttiness in our lives!

Peel the potato and slice it very thinly to ⅛-inch (3-mm) thickness, then slice it again to cut into matchsticks. Place the pieces in a colander and rinse them under running water several times to get rid of the surface starch. Drain. Sprinkle them with the salt and toss. Set them aside in the colander to continue to drain.

Slice the carrot and bell pepper into thin matchsticks.

In a skillet, heat the oil over medium heat. Add the potato, onion, carrot, bell pepper and garlic and stir-fry for 1 minute. Cover and let it simmer over low heat for 2 minutes. This will create steam in the skillet to cook the potato and the vegetables quickly.

Uncover it and stir gently, then season with salt and white pepper according to your taste. When the potato reaches the right texture of soft chewiness, 1 to 2 minutes (you'll have to test a few pieces as you cook), turn off the heat and sprinkle with the sesame seeds. Toss well to coat.

If you find that your potato is still too crunchy, cover it again and cook it a little longer until done, 1 to 2 minutes. Do not overcook to the point at which the potato matchsticks break easily. Serve hot or at room temperature as a side dish.

## (SHIGUMCHI MUCHIM, 시금치무침)

# SPINACH WITH TWO PASTES
## SERVES 2 TO 4

Salt

1 bunch fresh spinach, rinsed

2 tsp (11 g) Korean chili paste

2 tsp (11 g) Korean seasoned or fermented soybean paste

1 green onion, finely chopped

1 clove garlic, finely minced

2 tsp (10 ml) sesame oil

2 tsp (5 g) toasted sesame seeds

There are several different ways of dressing spinach as a side dish in Korean cooking. This gently spicy spinach side dish seasoned with two Korean fermented pastes has a rustic flavor that you would find at a countryside restaurant in the southern part of Korea. A hint of soybean paste (seasoned or plain) will add the robust flavor. It is my favorite way of enjoying spinach. If you are a fan of spinach, you can easily enjoy this alone with a bowl of rice as a light meal—no meat required!

Bring a pot of water to a boil over high heat. Add some salt and blanch the spinach for 10 seconds. Drain the spinach in a colander and rinse it with cold water until you cool down all the heat from the spinach.

Squeeze the moisture from the spinach, using both hands. If the spinach is too long, you can cut it to your desired length. Transfer the spinach to a bowl.

Add the chili paste, soybean paste, green onion, garlic, sesame oil and sesame seeds to the spinach. Rub the pastes together with your fingers to combine them first, and then massage all the ingredients into the spinach. Squeeze, turn and toss to incorporate the seasoning into the spinach, making sure all the strands of spinach are coated with the paste. Serve at room temperature or chill for 30 minutes.

**COOK'S TIP:** For convenience, wear disposable plastic gloves when you mix the spinach with the seasoning. Using finger massaging motions to season the vegetables with the seasoning sauce or paste is a distinctive technique of Korean cooking. Many vegetable dishes called namool use this mixing technique.

## WATERCRESS TOFU SALAD
### SERVES 4

8 oz (225 g) soft tofu

8 oz (225 g) watercress

Salt, divided

2 green onions, finely chopped

1 clove garlic, finely minced

1 tbsp (15 ml) Korean soy sauce for soup

2 tsp (10 ml) sesame oil

1 tbsp (8 g) toasted sesame seeds

**This elegant side salad is a vegan dieter's dream. It is healthy and unusually delicious, not to mention easy to put together. This is another so-called side dish that can easily turn into a meal of its own with a bowl of steamed rice.**

Bring a pot of water to a boil over high heat. Add the tofu and let it cook for 3 minutes. Remove the tofu, using a slotted spoon, and let it sit on a cutting board to cool down. Keep the water at a boil in the pot.

Add the watercress and pinches of salt to the boiling water and blanch the watercress for 1 minute. Remove the watercress with a strainer and rinse it with cold water several times. Squeeze the moisture from the watercress, then slice it to your desired length and place it in a bowl.

Using the side of a knife, smash the tofu into coarse crumbs. Collect the tofu crumbs and add them to the watercress.

Add the green onions, garlic, soy sauce for soup and sesame oil to the watercress. Toss with your hands to incorporate everything, using a massaging motion, shaking off the watercress to separate its leaves. Taste and adjust the seasoning by adding ¼ to ½ teaspoon of salt, if needed. Sprinkle with the sesame seeds and toss again. Serve this salad chilled or at room temperature.

## (MAYAK GYERAN, 마약계란)

## ADDICTIVE SOY SAUCE EGGS
### MAKES 12 EGGS

1 dozen eggs

1 tbsp (18 g) salt

1 tbsp (15 ml) vinegar

1 cup (240 ml) soy sauce

1 cup (240 ml) water

½ cup (120 ml) Korean oligo syrup or corn syrup

½ cup (100 g) sugar

2 green onions, finely chopped

1 red chile, minced

1 tbsp (10 g) minced garlic

2 tbsp (16 g) toasted sesame seeds

Steamed rice, for serving

Like the ubiquitous avocado toast that U.S. millennials seem to be obsessed with, this egg dish has gone viral on Korean social networks. Soft-boiled eggs are marinated in a soy sauce mixture that flavors the eggs on the outside. The silky, smooth egg yolks and the flavorful marinade do a wonderful job of dressing up plain rice. You can affect how soft your egg yolks will be by adjusting the simmering time. Some like their eggs almost hard-boiled, whereas others prefer very runny yolks. I like mine in between.

Place the eggs in a large pan. Add the salt, vinegar and enough water to cover the eggs. Bring them to a boil over medium-high heat. Once the water is boiling, cover, lower the heat to medium and simmer for 8 minutes to yield soft-boiled eggs. Remove the eggs from the water and place them in cold water to cool completely. Peel away the shells and set the eggs aside.

In the meantime, in a large bowl, combine the soy sauce, 1 cup (240 ml) of fresh water, the syrup, sugar, green onions, chile, garlic and sesame seeds in a large bowl and stir together until the sugar dissolves completely.

Add the eggs and cover. Chill in the fridge for at least 4 hours to overnight, turning the eggs occasionally to ensure they marinate evenly.

To serve, cut each egg in half and place it on top of steamed rice. Drizzle the marinade over the eggs and rice.

**COOK'S TIP:** If you prefer your eggs to be hard-boiled, cook them for 11 to 12 minutes. For looser egg yolks, cook for 7 to 7½ minutes.

## (DALGYAL JJIM, 달걀찜)

## STEAMED EGG PUDDING
### SERVES 4

5 large eggs

About 1 cup (240 ml) chicken stock

1 tsp Korean salted shrimp, chopped

Salt

Oil, for brushing

1 green onion, finely chopped

1 tsp toasted sesame seeds

**Velvety soft and smooth, dalgyal jjim (or gyeran jjim) is one of the most sought-after side dishes people expect in Korean restaurants. Just remember, this is a savory pudding, so don't expect this to be like a sweet custard or flan. Also, it is extremely hot when served, so be careful not to burn your tongue. To enjoy the soft and moist pudding, the best ratio of egg to liquid (chicken stock) is 1:1 by volume. A tiny bit of salted shrimp adds a good flavor to the dish, so don't skip that.**

In a medium bowl, whisk together the eggs and an equal volume of chicken stock. Add the salted shrimp and salt to taste; mix well.

Using a brush, oil a 1-quart (1-L) pot and heat it over medium heat. Pour in the egg mixture, stirring constantly, until the egg starts to bubble up and expand, 3 to 4 minutes. When the egg is about 80 percent cooked, 1 to 2 minutes, cover it and lower the heat to medium-low, then cook for 2 to 3 more minutes. The egg will expand slightly toward the top of the pot.

Using a hot pad or oven mitt, uncover the pot. Be careful; the lid will be very hot. Sprinkle the green onion and sesame seeds on top of the pudding. Serve hot. The pudding will deflate as it cools.

**COOK'S TIP:** If you would like to enjoy a silkier pudding, strain the egg mixture through a fine strainer to remove the albumen (the white stringy part of the egg white) before adding it to the pot.

**( OOI MUCHIM, 오이무침 )**

# SPICY CUCUMBER SALAD
## SERVES 4 TO 6

1 English, 2 Korean or 2 Kirby cucumbers

1 tbsp (16 g) Korean chili paste

1 tbsp (6 g) Korean chili flakes

1 tbsp (13 g) sugar

1 tbsp (15 ml) rice vinegar

1 clove garlic, finely minced

Salt

½ small onion, thinly sliced

1 tbsp (8 g) toasted sesame seeds

1 tbsp (3 g) chopped fresh cilantro (optional)

If you need a quick side salad to serve with your Korean barbecue, look no further. This spicy cucumber salad can be made in less than ten minutes. Crunchy and cool, this will be a perfect side dish to go with any Korean meal. You can use either Korean cucumber, or Kirby or English cucumber. They are all delicious. Although it is untraditional, I like to add a little bit of fresh cilantro at the end. I think the fragrance of the cilantro goes really well with the Korean chili paste.

Cut the cucumber in half lengthwise, and then slice each half thinly (diagonally if desired), making semicircular disks; set aside.

In a large bowl, combine the chili paste, chili flakes, sugar, vinegar, garlic and a pinch of salt and mix well.

Add the cucumber and onion to the seasoning paste and toss well with a spoon. Taste and add more salt or chili paste according to your taste. Sprinkle with the sesame seeds and fresh cilantro, if using. Serve immediately.

**COOK'S TIP:** Once seasoned, cucumbers will release lots of moisture over time, thinning out the dressing and making the salad watery. If you need to make this ahead of time, store the sliced cucumber and onion and the dressing in separate containers in the fridge, then toss everything together right before you serve.

**(JANGJORIM, 장조림)**

## SOY-BRAISED SHREDDED BEEF & CHILES

### SERVES 4 TO 6

1¼ lb (567 g) beef brisket or flank steak

½ onion

4 to 5 cloves garlic

8 to 10 whole peppercorns (optional)

2.5 oz (70 g) shishito chile or other mild chiles (optional)

7 tbsp (105 ml) soy sauce

3 tbsp (39 g) sugar

3 tbsp (45 ml) sweet rice wine (mirin)

**Beef brisket is commonly used for this delicious side dish, but other cuts, such as flank steak or eye round steak, can also be used. Traditionally, hard-boiled quail eggs are often added at the end of cooking, but I like to add fresh mild chiles to mine. They give a refreshing flavor to the beef, but it is optional. Braising in soy sauce at the end of cooking makes the beef very tender and soft.**

In a large pot, combine the beef, onion, garlic and peppercorns, if using, and pour in enough water to cover them. Bring it to a gentle boil, then simmer it over low heat for 45 minutes, or until the beef is soft and tender. Remove the beef from the pot. Reserve 1½ cups (360 ml) of the hot broth.

Let the beef cool for 10 minutes, then shred it into bite-size pieces. Set aside.

If using the chiles poke them with a fork a couple of times, front and back. Set aside.

In the same pot as used before, combine the reserved beef broth, soy sauce, sugar and rice wine and mix well. Bring them to a full boil.

Add the beef and the chile. Lower the heat to low and simmer for 5 minutes. Remove it from the heat and let everything cool in the pot. Store the beef in the fridge for up to 2 weeks. Serve hot, at room temperature or cold.

**COOK'S TIP:** Once chilled, you might see tiny white fat particles floating in the broth. If that bothers you, microwave for 10 to 20 seconds to melt them off.

## MASHED KABOCHA SQUASH & SWEET POTATO SALAD

**SERVES 6**

½ kabocha squash, about 21 oz (600 g), seeded and diced

1 large sweet potato (preferably Korean sweet potato), about 12 oz (340 g), diced

¼ cup (55 g) mayonnaise

2 tbsp (30 g) light brown sugar

1 tbsp (16 g) prepared yellow mustard

¼ tsp salt

2 tbsp (30 ml) heavy cream or whole milk

¼ cup (35 g) raisins

¼ cup (28 g) finely chopped pecans

On a recent trip to Korea, I discovered that many upscale restaurants are serving this delightful kabocha squash salad as a side dish. You must use kabocha squash for this recipe. Other types of winter squash have too much moisture and just won't work as well. I also recommend using Korean sweet potatoes to give the salad a thicker texture. Both can be found in many Asian markets in the fall and winter. With the intense orange flesh of the squash, this salad is beautiful, tasty and very healthy. Despite its rough texture when raw, the kabocha squash rind becomes soft enough to eat when cooked. It is high in fiber, vitamins and minerals.

Heat a steamer over medium-high heat. Place the squash and sweet potato in the steamer and steam them until they are fork-tender, 10 to 15 minutes. The sweet potato will take longer to steam.

Transfer the squash and potato pieces to a bowl. Mash them together, using a potato masher or fork, leaving a few tiny chunks, if you wish. Add the mayonnaise, sugar, mustard, salt, cream and raisins and mix well. Add the pecans and mix briefly. Chill the salad for at least 30 minutes before you serve.

3 tbsp (24 g) toasted black sesame seeds
5 tbsp (75 ml) whole milk
3 tbsp (38 g) Greek yogurt
¼ cup (55 g) mayonnaise
1 tbsp (13 g) sugar
1½ tbsp (23 ml) fresh lemon juice
⅛ tsp salt
Assorted salad vegetables, including iceberg lettuce, spring greens, cucumber and cherry tomatoes

# GREEN SALAD WITH BLACK SESAME DRESSING
## MAKES 1½ CUPS (360 ML) DRESSING

**Many upscale Korean restaurants serve this type of green salad with a dressing made of black sesame seeds. The creamy dressing over cold salad vegetables is so refreshing before the main course arrives. A big chunk of iceberg lettuce in your salad provides a delightfully crisp texture. I recommend washing and spinning your salad greens ahead of time, then chilling them again in the fridge to ensure they are nice and crispy come mealtime. Lifeless greens just won't do for this salad.**

Using a spice grinder, mini blender or mortar and pestle, grind the black sesame seeds.

In a small bowl, whisk together the ground sesame seeds, milk, yogurt, mayonnaise, sugar, lemon juice and salt.

Drizzle the dressing over the salad mixture right away or chill it in the fridge until mealtime. The dressing will stay fresh for 2 weeks in the fridge.

**(GIMGUI, 김구이)**

# HOMEMADE ROASTED SEAWEED
## MAKES 30 SHEETS

1 tbsp (15 ml) olive oil

1 tbsp (15 ml) wild sesame or sesame oil

30 sheets unroasted and unseasoned seaweed (see Cook's Tips)

Kosher salt

Sure, you can easily purchase packaged roasted seaweed in many grocery stores these days. Roasting your own seaweed at home, though, is totally worth it. If you're intimidated by that idea, then just read on. You can roast 30 sheets of seaweed on your own stove in less than 20 minutes. You can't beat the fresh taste of homemade roasted seaweed and it's so much better for you. Enjoy wrapping hot rice with the seaweed or eating it alone as a healthy snack.

In a small bowl, mix together the olive and wild sesame oils.

Set aside a dry baking sheet. Lay a seaweed sheet on a cutting board. With a disposable plastic glove on one hand, dip a couple of fingers into the oils. Make a fist with your fingers to coat your palm with the oil and then dab it onto the seaweed sheet to lightly coat it with oil. Try to move quickly but gently without tearing the seaweed. Don't use too much oil. With the other dry hand, evenly sprinkle a pinch of salt over the oiled seaweed. Set the seaweed aside on the baking sheet. Repeat with the rest of the seaweed.

Heat a large skillet or griddle over medium heat until hot. Using tongs, transfer 2 sheets of seaweed, one on top of the other, to the hot skillet. The seaweed will shrink within a few seconds. Turn it to the other side and continue to roast for a few more seconds. The seaweed will have a dark green hue on the surface and become crisp. If golden brown spots appear on the seaweed's surface, the heat is too high; adjust the heat accordingly as needed. Remove it from the skillet and let it cool completely.

Cut each seaweed sheet into 8 segments and put them in an airtight container lined with a paper towel on the bottom. Store at room temperature up to 3 days, or longer in the freezer.

**COOK'S TIPS:** Look for unroasted and unseasoned seaweed called gim that is thin but has a coarse texture. The seaweed should be black in color, with maybe a hint of green, and it usually sells in packages of 50 or 100 sheets. Avoid seaweed sheets that have a red or purple tint, because that usually means that the seaweed has gone rancid. Store your seaweed in a freezer.

When roasted seaweed loses its crispiness, you can bring it back to life by putting it on a paper towel–lined microwave-safe plate and microwaving it for 10 to 15 seconds.

# ALMIGHTY
## KIMCHI

**KIMCHI** is a hallmark of Korean cuisine. There are over 200 recognized varieties of kimchi—which means that pretty much anything that sprouts on this planet can be made into kimchi. In addition to its taste, the well-documented health benefits of fermentation provide motivation to make kimchi at home. Success in making good kimchi relies on both salt brining and fermenting.

In the olden days, Koreans buried their kimchi underground in large stone urns to maintain a consistent temperature during winter. However, most Korean households these days own a separate refrigerator that is specially designed for storing and fermenting kimchi. Kimchi ferments most ideally at 41 to 45°F (5 to 7°C), depending on the type of kimchi. Once fermented, it needs a very cool temperature (32 to 34°F [0 to 1°C]) to maintain its ideal flavor. This is slightly colder than most common household refrigerators, but not cold enough to freeze the kimchi.

Not everyone has the luxury of owning a separate refrigerator just for kimchi, but there are some tricks you can use to prolong the life of your kimchi. Here are a few tips:

**1.** Use an airtight container. Air is the number one enemy to the kimchi fermenting process.

**2.** Place your kimchi in the coldest section in your fridge, but be careful not to lower the temperature of your refrigerator too much.

**3.** Do not make too much kimchi at once unless you intend to use the overly fermented kimchi for making stews or some other purpose. If you make a large amount of kimchi, store it divided among several small containers to avoid frequent exposure to the air.

**4.** If your kimchi gets sour quickly, add clean eggshells or green tea bags to your kimchi container. The alkali character of these ingredients will slow down the fast process of fermenting and reduce its acidity.

In this chapter, you will find many unique kimchi varieties that are delicious and easy to make.

## (BAECHU KIMCHI, 배추김치)

4½ lb (2 kg) napa cabbage

⅔ cup (140 g) coarse sea salt, preferably Korean origin

### KIMCHI STOCK

1 sweet apple, seeded and thinly sliced

½ Asian pear, seeded and thinly sliced

1 (4" [10-cm]) piece dried sea kelp

1 leek, diced

2 cups (480 ml) water

### KIMCHI PASTE

1 cup (240 ml) kimchi stock

½ large onion, diced

10 cloves garlic

1 (1" [2.5-cm]) piece fresh ginger, peeled and diced

2 tbsp (21 g) cooked white rice

2 tbsp (26 g) Korean salted shrimp

¼ cup (60 ml) Korean anchovy sauce

1 tbsp (13 g) sugar

3.5 oz (100 g) Korean chili flakes

4 oz (115 g) Asian chives or green onion, sliced (optional)

**COOK'S TIP:** If you'd like to enjoy freshly made, unfermented cabbage kimchi in the authentic Korean way on the same day you made it, leave a small portion of kimchi (enough for a meal) in the mixing bowl. Add 1 to 2 teaspoons of sesame oil and toasted sesame seeds; toss well. Serve with soybean paste stew, braised pork belly or noodle soup. Divine!

# EASY AUTHENTIC CABBAGE KIMCHI
## MAKES ABOUT 5 PINTS (2.3 L) KIMCHI

Making traditional cabbage kimchi takes some time and skill, but here is an easy version. Good kimchi needs starch to feed the good bacteria, which helps the fermentation. Traditional, authentic kimchi requires rice flour paste; however, I'll share my mother's trick for this type of kimchi, which is to use leftover rice! Also, don't skip the kimchi stock. It takes the flavor of your kimchi to a higher level.

Separate the cabbage leaves from their core. Rinse the cabbage leaves once. Slice each leaf into 2-inch (5-cm) slices.

In a very large mixing bowl (or use your kitchen sink with the drain closed), place a thin layer of cabbage pieces and sprinkle evenly with 2 tablespoons (36 g) of sea salt. Layer more cabbage on top and sprinkle with salt. Repeat the layers. Let the layered, salted cabbage sit for 1½ hours, or until the leaves are all well brined. You will need to turn the cabbage from top to bottom a couple of times during the brining so that they are evenly salted. You know that the cabbage is well salted if you can bend the stem of the cabbage without breaking it. Rinse 3 times and drain the leaves in a colander to remove extra moisture.

For the kimchi stock, in a small pot, combine the apple, pear, dried sea kelp, leek and water and bring it to a boil over high heat. Remove the sea kelp and lower the heat to low; simmer for 5 minutes. Reserve 1 cup (240 ml) of the stock.

To prepare the kimchi paste, in a blender, combine the reserved kimchi stock, onion, garlic, ginger, rice and salted shrimp and process until very smooth. Pour the mixture into a medium bowl and add the anchovy sauce, sugar and Korean chili flakes; mix well. Let the paste sit for 5 minutes.

Transfer the cabbage to a very large, shallow bowl. Add the chives (if using) and the kimchi paste to the cabbage. Make sure you wear a pair of rubber or plastic kitchen gloves to protect your delicate hands. Toss well so that the cabbage pieces are well covered with the paste.

Transfer the kimchi to an airtight 3-quart (3-L) container. If you wish to have more kimchi liquid, add about 1 cup (240 ml) water to the mixing bowl, swirl around to collect the entire paste residue inside and pour the mixture into the kimchi container. Seal the container.

To ferment the kimchi, let your kimchi sit on the counter for 1 to 2 days, depending on your room temperature. Then, place it in the fridge and let it continue to ferment for another 2 to 3 days.

## (MOO KIMCHI, 무김치)

Scant 4½ lb (2 kg) Korean radish (about 2 medium radishes)

⅓ cup (70 g) Korean coarse sea salt

⅓ cup (67 g) + 1½ tbsp (19 g) sugar, divided

½ large onion, diced

6 cloves garlic

1 (1" [2.5-cm]) piece fresh ginger, peeled and chopped

3 tbsp (39 g) Korean salted shrimp

2 tbsp (30 ml) Korean anchovy sauce

⅓ cup (80 ml) whole milk

½ cup (50 g) Korean chili flakes

1 Asian leek or 3 green onions, chopped

# MAKES ABOUT 3 PINTS (1.4 L) KIMCHI

Along with cabbage kimchi, radish kimchi is another well-known and popular kimchi for all Korean food lovers. This "level 101" kimchi is easier and quicker to make than cabbage kimchi—but you must use a Korean radish to maintain the crunchiness. Here I share with you a secret to make the radish kimchi even tastier: add a small amount of milk. Yes, milk! Milk will help in the formation of gas during the fermentation stage. It won't curdle but will provide a very good flavor to the kimchi. You won't taste or smell the milk at all. I am sure you will be happy with the resulting crunchy, refreshing and perfectly fermented radish kimchi.

Peel the radishes and slice them into ¾-inch (2-cm)-thick disks. Quarter each disk to create large bite-size pieces. Put the radish slices in a large mixing bowl. Add the salt and ⅓ cup (67 g) of sugar, then toss well and set aside for 1 hour.

Rinse the radish slices once and put them in a colander to drain off the extra water; set aside.

In a blender, combine the onion, garlic, ginger, salted shrimp, anchovy sauce and milk until very smooth. Pour the puree into a medium bowl. Add the chili flakes and 1½ tablespoons (19 g) of sugar; mix well and set aside for 5 to 10 minutes to let the chili flakes absorb the moisture.

Return the radishes to the large bowl and add the leek and the chili mixture. Wearing disposable plastic gloves, toss the mixture together with your hands to coat the radishes with the chili mixture. Transfer it to an airtight 2-quart (2-L) container.

This is optional, but if you like to have more kimchi liquid, put ½ to 1 cup (120 to 240 ml) of water into the bowl you tossed the kimchi in, and wipe all the kimchi residue remaining in the bowl into the water. Pour the liquid over the radish kimchi in its airtight container and close it tightly.

Let the kimchi sit in its airtight container at room temperature for 2 days, and then transfer it to the refrigerator to continue to ferment for another 3 to 5 days. Serve the radish kimchi chilled.

**COOK'S TIP:** Radish kimchi will release lots of its juice as it ferments. Do not throw away the liquid even when you finish the entire kimchi. Collect the juice in a glass jar and store it in the refrigerator. You can add the juice to your kimchi stew, kimchi fried rice, kimchi pancakes or anything you make with kimchi to enhance the flavor.

2½ lb (1.1 kg) Korean or Kirby cucumbers

4 cups (960 ml) water

¼ cup (52 g) Korean coarse sea salt

½ large onion

2 cloves garlic

1 (½" [1.3-cm]) piece fresh ginger

2 tbsp (30 ml) Korean anchovy sauce

1 tbsp (13 g) Korean salted shrimp

2 tbsp (30 ml) Korean plum extract (optional)

½ cup (50 g) Korean chili flakes

1 tbsp (13 g) sugar

¾ cup (90 g) finely chopped Asian chives or green onion

# CUCUMBER KIMCHI
## MAKES ABOUT 4 PINTS (1.9 L) KIMCHI

With its cool and refreshing texture, cucumber kimchi is the kimchi of summer in Korea. The secret to long-lasting crunchiness, even after the fermentation, is to brine the cucumbers . . . in boiling salted water! Don't worry, it won't cook the cucumbers and they won't be mushy. You will enjoy the crisp crunchiness in every bite all the way until you finish the entire batch. If you can't find Korean cucumbers, look for Kirby cucumbers. The typical waxy American cucumbers are not suitable for kimchi.

Leaving about an inch (2.5 cm) uncut on each end of a cucumber, cut a slit all the way through the cucumber. Then, turn the cucumber 90 degrees and cut again all the way through the cucumber, again leaving about an inch (2.5 cm) uncut at either end. Repeat for all the cucumbers and place them in a large, heatproof bowl.

Meanwhile, in a pot, bring the water and salt to a full boil. The salt should be completely dissolved. Pour the salted boiling water over the cucumbers and stir well. Let it sit for 40 minutes, tossing the cucumbers once or twice during the brining. Drain the water and rinse the cucumbers with cold water once. Place them in a colander to drain.

In a blender, combine the onion, garlic, ginger, anchovy sauce, salted shrimp and plum extract, if using, and blend until smooth. Transfer the mixture to a bowl. Add the chili flakes, sugar and chives and mix well.

Using a spoon, stuff a generous amount of the chive filling into the slits you have cut in the cucumber pieces. Put the cucumber kimchi in an airtight 3-quart (3-L) container. To ferment, let the kimchi sit at room temperature for 1 day, then store it in a refrigerator. Cucumber kimchi will last for about 3 weeks in the fridge. Cut the kimchi into bite-size disks to serve.

**COOK'S TIP:** If you prepare this kimchi during the hot summer and your kitchen is not air-conditioned, you might only need a half day of letting your kimchi sit at room temperature. Check by tasting a piece of kimchi. It should have a pungent and fermented flavor. After you put the kimchi in the refrigerator, it will continue to ferment slowly. Within 2 to 3 days, this cucumber kimchi should be ready to serve.

## (GUNDAE KIMCHI, 근대김치)

1 bunch (10 oz [275 g]) Swiss chard

¼ cup (52 g) Korean coarse sea salt, divided

1 lb (455 g) Korean radish, peeled

1½ tbsp (15 g) sweet rice flour

1 cup (240 ml) water

6 tbsp (38 g) Korean chili flakes

1 tbsp (13 g) sugar

3 tbsp (45 ml) Korean anchovy sauce

4 cloves garlic, minced

2 tsp (10 ml) pureed fresh ginger

1 bunch green onions, sliced

# SWISS CHARD KIMCHI
## MAKES ABOUT 3 PINTS (1.4 L) KIMCHI

**Big, leafy Swiss chard is perfect for making kimchi. The radish slices in between the Swiss chard leaves add a delicious crunchiness. It is fun to lift up a leaf of Swiss chard kimchi and wrap it around a mouthful of hot cooked rice. This kimchi is perfect for wintertime when Swiss chard is at its tender best. This type of quick kimchi is not meant to be stored for a long period of time, so try to consume it within a couple of weeks—although I don't think it will go uneaten for that long!**

Rinse the Swiss chard under running water and place it in a large bowl. Sprinkle 3 tablespoons (75 g) of sea salt on the wet leaves and let them sit until they wilt a little, about 25 minutes. If needed, sprinkle some water on each leaf to dissolve the salt faster.

Slice the Korean radish thinly and cut it into matchsticks less than ⅛ inch (3 mm) thick. Sprinkle the remaining 1 tablespoon (25 g) of sea salt on the radish and toss. Set aside until the radish wilts, about 10 minutes.

Meanwhile, to make rice flour paste, in a small pot, whisk the sweet rice flour into the fresh water over medium-high heat and bring it to a boil. Whisk constantly until the mixture thickens, 2 to 3 minutes. Remove it from the heat and let it cool.

Rinse the radish once and squeeze out the extra moisture. Place the radish in a large bowl, add the chili flakes, sugar, anchovy sauce, garlic, ginger, green onions and sweet rice flour paste. Mix well with a wooden spoon until the radish slices are covered with a thin paste; set aside.

Rinse the Swiss chard by swirling the leaves just once in a big bowl of water and place them in a colander. Set aside to drain.

On a baking sheet or large platter, spread 1 leaf of Swiss chard flat. Evenly spread about 2 to 3 tablespoons (20 to 30 g) of radish filling on the leaf. Add another layer of Swiss chard and filling and repeat, 1 leaf at a time, until the last leaf on top is covered with the filling.

Cut the multilayered Swiss chard kimchi into 3 to 5 sections, depending on the size you desire. Transfer them into an airtight 2-quart (2-L) container. Keep the kimchi at room temperature for a day. The kimchi is ready to serve from the day you made it. You can store the kimchi in a refrigerator for up to 2 weeks, where it will continue to slowly ferment. Unlike cabbage kimchi, this kimchi is not meant to be overly fermented—so don't hesitate to eat it all within 2 weeks.

## (GOSU KIMCHI, 고수김치)

1 cup (240 ml) water

1 tbsp (10 g) sweet rice flour

3 bunches (about 8.4 oz [238 g] total) fresh cilantro

1 bunch green onions

⅓ cup (33 g) Korean chili flakes

3 cloves garlic, finely minced

2 tsp (10 ml) pureed fresh ginger

3 tbsp (45 ml) Korean tuna or anchovy sauce

1 tbsp (13 g) sugar

1 to 2 fresh red chiles, sliced (optional)

# CILANTRO KIMCHI
## MAKES ABOUT 3 PINTS (1.4 L) KIMCHI

Cilantro is not a common herb in Korean cuisine, but it is not unheard of, either. Interestingly, since cilantro is believed to be a detoxifying herb, you will often find salad dishes made with cilantro at Buddhist temples in South Korea. It is more commonly eaten in North Korea, however. I have discovered that cilantro makes wonderful kimchi. The unique but strong fragrance of cilantro subsides as it ferments and becomes a very enjoyable kimchi. You can enjoy this kimchi fresh on the day you make it, or fermented. As a bonus, this kimchi is perhaps the easiest and quickest kimchi you can make. It will only take ten minutes from start to finish. I love that.

To make rice flour paste, in a small pot, whisk together the water and rice flour over medium-high heat and bring it to a boil. Whisk constantly until the mixture thickens, 2 to 3 minutes. Remove it from the heat and set it aside to cool.

Rinse and drain the cilantro in a colander; set aside.

Cut the green onions in half lengthwise and slice them into pieces about 2 inches (5 cm) in length.

In a large bowl, mix together the rice flour paste, chili flakes, garlic, ginger, tuna sauce, sugar and red chile, if using. Let the paste rest for 5 minutes.

Add the cilantro and the green onions and toss with your hands or kitchen tongs to incorporate. The cilantro will wilt very quickly. Transfer the kimchi to an airtight 1-quart (1-L) container. Enjoy the kimchi fresh, or let it sit at room temperature for a day and then store it in the fridge for another 3 to 5 days to ferment to your preferred taste.

**COOK'S TIP:** Fresh cilantro is often served alongside grilled pork belly in many Korean restaurants. Try serving this cilantro kimchi on top of your favorite Korean barbecued meat, wrapped in lettuce.

## (CHEONGGYOUNGCHAE GAM KIMCHI, 청경채감김치)

2½ lb (1.1 kg) bok choy, halved or quartered lengthwise

½ cup (105 g) Korean coarse sea salt

1½ tbsp (15 g) sweet rice flour

½ cup (120 ml) water

1 very ripe hongsi persimmon

1 small onion, diced

3 tbsp (45 ml) Korean anchovy sauce

1 tbsp (13 g) Korean salted shrimp

4 cloves garlic

1 (½" [1.3-cm]) piece fresh ginger piece, peeled and diced

4 to 5 fresh finger-long red chiles, diced

½ cup (50 g) Korean chili flakes

# BOK CHOY PERSIMMON KIMCHI
## MAKES ABOUT 3 PINTS (1.4 L) KIMCHI

Persimmons are a common winter fruit in Korea. Luckily, you can find persimmons easily in many upscale grocery stores these days. There are two types: hongsi has a tall and elongated shape and ripens to a sweet jellylike texture; yeonsi is short and slightly square in shape, and is firm and crunchy. The well-ripened sweet hongsi persimmon is wonderful to add to kimchi. It goes really well with the tender crispiness of bok choy and you will love the sweet flavor. This is a very easy kimchi to make and you can put it together fairly quickly. Most of the time, hongsi persimmons at the store are not perfectly soft and ripe, so make sure to let your hongsi ripen on the counter until they become very soft and jelly-like. It might take several days.

Rinse the bok choy with water and lay a few pieces in a single layer in a large bowl. Evenly sprinkle some sea salt on top. Add another layer of bok choy and sprinkle with the salt. Repeat until all the bok choy is layered and salted. Let it sit for 30 minutes, then turn over the bok choy so that all layers soak evenly in the brine. Let it sit for another 30 minutes. Rinse the bok choy a couple of times with water and gently squeeze out the extra moisture. Place it in a strainer to drain; set aside.

In the meantime, make the rice flour paste. In a small pot, whisk together the rice flour and water over medium-high heat and bring it to a boil. Whisk constantly until the mixture thickens, 2 to 3 minutes. Remove it from the heat and set it aside to cool.

Remove the stem from the persimmon and slice the fruit in half lengthwise. Cut out the fibrous core of the persimmon, and scoop out all the jelly-like pulp with a spoon. Discard the persimmon skin.

In a blender, combine the persimmon pulp, onion, anchovy sauce, salted shrimp, garlic, ginger and rice flour paste and blend until smooth. Add the fresh chiles and pulse a few times so that you get the small chunks of chiles in the puree.

Pour the persimmon mixture into a bowl and add the chili flakes; mix well and let it sit for 5 minutes.

Add the bok choy to the kimchi paste and, wearing disposable plastic gloves, toss gently, using your hands.

You can serve the freshly made bok choy kimchi on the same day you made it, to enjoy the tender and crisp texture of bok choy. If you prefer to let it ferment, put the bok choy kimchi in an airtight 2-quart (2-L) container and let it sit at room temperature for 1 day, and then transfer the kimchi to a fridge and ferment for another 3 to 4 days. It will keep in the fridge for 2 to 3 weeks.

## (AGI KIMCHI, 아기김치)

## MILD GREEN CABBAGE KIMCHI

### MAKES ABOUT 3 PINTS (1.4 L) KIMCHI

1 green cabbage (about 1¾ lb [794 g]), cored and diced

¼ cup (50 g) Korean coarse sea salt

2 red bell peppers, seeded, cored and cut into chunks

½ large onion, diced

½ red sweet apple, seeded and diced

4 cloves garlic

1 (1" (2.5-cm) piece fresh ginger, peeled and chopped

1 tbsp (13 g) sugar

2 tbsp (20 g) cooked white rice

2 tbsp (26 g) Korean salted shrimp

3 tbsp (45 ml) Korean tuna sauce or anchovy sauce

1 bunch green onions, sliced

1 to 2 tsp (3 to 6 g) black sesame seeds, for garnish (optional)

*Agi* means "baby" in Korean; therefore, as you can tell, this nonspicy kimchi is created to introduce kimchi to children who can't handle the spiciness yet. However, please don't think that this kimchi is limited only to them. People of all ages (and those who are kids at heart) can enjoy this delicious kimchi. Crunchy green cabbage is perfect to make kimchi with. Sweet and mild red bell pepper replaces the red chile, and once fermented, it offers refreshingly clean flavors. This is an extremely easy kimchi that anyone can make.

Rinse the diced cabbage pieces with water and put them in a large bowl. Sprinkle them with the sea salt and toss well. Let it sit for 45 to 60 minutes, tossing once midway through. Once the cabbage is slightly wilted, rinse it again with water once and place it in a strainer to drain all the water.

In a blender, combine the bell peppers, onion, apple, garlic, ginger, sugar, rice, salted shrimp and tuna sauce and blend until smooth. Add a little water for the blade to run, if needed.

In a large bowl, combine the cabbage, green onions and bell pepper puree and toss well. Put the kimchi in an airtight 2-quart (2-L) container. Let it sit at room temperature for 2 days, and then continue to ferment in the fridge for 4 to 5 days for perfectly fermented kimchi. This kimchi will retain its crispness in the fridge for up to 1 month.

Garnish with sesame seeds before serving, if desired.

**COOK'S TIP:** If you cook a batch of white rice (preferably short-grain rice) for your meal, freeze some leftover rice in several freezer bags for later use for kimchi making. All you need is to reheat the cooked rice in a microwave and blend it with the other ingredients in kimchi. It saves the extra step of making rice flour paste, which is an essential component in kimchi fermentation.

# SWEET
# TREATS
# & DRINKS

**TRADITIONAL** Korean cuisine is not big on desserts. With many decades of social and political influence from other cultures, however, Korean desserts have evolved to the point that there is now a wide variety of sweet treats that are unique to Korea, and many people are falling in love with them.

Who wouldn't love a hot, crisp-yet-chewy sticky bun filled with warm sweet cinnamon sugar filling inside (page 162)? If that is not indulgent enough, how about soft, melt-in-your-mouth donuts (page 165)? If those seem too heavy, then consider a light refreshment in the form of fruity shaved ice (page 170) or a lemony beverage (page 174)? Either one is a light way to finish off a heavy meal and cool down on a hot summer day. In the winter, the soul-comforting spiced tea (page 173) is a perfect way to sooth your mind and body.

Whether you want to serve these treats and drinks as a finale to your Korean feast or just indulge in them on their own, they won't disappoint.

## (HOTTEOK, 호떡)

# SWEET PANCAKES WITH CINNAMON BROWN SUGAR FILLING

## MAKES ABOUT 8 TO 10 HOTTEOK

### DOUGH

2½ cups (313 g) all-purpose flour

½ cup (79 g) sweet rice flour

1 tsp sugar

1 tsp salt

2 tsp (8 g) instant yeast

½ tsp baking powder

1¼ cups (300 ml) whole milk, lukewarm

3 tbsp (42 g) unsalted butter, melted

Oil, for hands and frying

### CINNAMON BROWN SUGAR FILLING

⅔ cup (150 g) light brown sugar

1 tsp ground cinnamon

½ tbsp (4 g) all-purpose flour

¼ cup (35 g) finely chopped roasted peanuts

**Step aside, cinnamon buns. Nobody can resist these hot fried pancakes filled with oozing sweet cinnamon sugar. Hotteok is the most well-known Korean sweet treat. There are many recipes available online but nothing will be superior to this one for its soft and chewy, yet crisp dough texture. Don't skip the sweet rice flour. It will enhance the chewiness of the dough. A little bit of baking powder will make the bun very soft as well.**

In a large bowl, stir together the flours, sugar, salt, yeast and baking powder. Pour in the milk and the melted butter; mix well with a wooden spoon. Continue to stir the dough with the wooden spoon for 2 minutes to develop the gluten.

Cover the dough with a damp towel and let it sit in a warm place for 1 to 2 hours, or until it's doubled in volume.

Meanwhile, prepare the filling. In a bowl, mix together the brown sugar, cinnamon, flour and peanuts. Set aside.

When the dough has doubled in volume, punch down the dough and let it rest for a few more minutes. Keep a small bowl with a little bit of oil on the side to oil your hands.

On a griddle, heat 2 tablespoons (30 ml) of oil over medium-low heat. Oil your hands, take a piece of the dough (about one-eighth to one-tenth of the total amount) and flatten it in your palm. Using a round spoon, place a heaping tablespoon (18 g) of the filling in the center of the dough. Gather the dough around the filling and pinch it to seal the filling inside.

Place the dough seam side down on the hot griddle and let it sear for 30 seconds. Flip the dough to the other side and press down with a greased hotteok press or spatula to flatten it to about a ½-inch (1.3-cm) thickness. Do not press down too much; if it gets too thin, the dough will tear easily. Panfry for 1 to 2 minutes, or until it's golden brown. Then, flip to the other side again and continue to cook until it's golden brown and crisp. Drizzle more oil on the griddle, as needed, and adjust the heat level so that you don't brown the crust too quickly. Repeat to cook the remaining dough.

Serve hot and be careful not to burn your tongue.

## (KWABAEGI DONUTS, 꽈배기도넛)

2⅔ cups (365 g) bread flour, plus more for dusting

½ cup (45 g) cake flour

½ tsp salt

3 tbsp (39 g) sugar

½ tsp freshly grated nutmeg

2 tsp (8 g) instant yeast

1 large egg

2 tbsp (28 g) unsalted butter, melted and cooled

1 cup (240 ml) lukewarm whole milk

Oil, for bowl and deep-frying

### CINNAMON-SUGAR COATING

½ cup (100 g) sugar

1 tbsp (8 g) ground cinnamon

# KOREAN TWISTED DONUTS
## MAKES 16 DONUTS

I made these donuts one rainy day and wanted to share them with a family we know. I asked my teenage son to deliver them to the family, and told him to tell the family these are Korean donuts. When my son handed the donuts to them at their door, they asked him what made these Korean. He responded, "Well, a Korean lady made them, so they are Korean donuts!" Even though there is no special Korean ingredient in the recipe, these are the donuts you will see on the corner of every street market in Korea. So, indeed, they are 100 percent Korean. What's more, my son the donut expert gives these two thumbs up!

In the bowl of an electric mixer or a large bowl, combine the flours, salt, sugar, nutmeg and yeast; stir well with a wooden spoon. Add the egg, melted butter and milk; mix well with a wooden spoon so the mixture will come together.

Attach the dough hook and knead the dough on a medium speed for 3 minutes, or knead by hand for 5 minutes, or until the dough becomes soft and stretchy. Form the dough into a smooth ball and place it in an oiled bowl. Cover it with a damp, clean towel and let the dough rise in a warm place for 1 hour, or until it's doubled in volume.

Punch down the dough and place it on a cutting board dusted with flour. Divide the dough into 16 pieces. Using the palms of your hands, roll each piece of dough into a 10-inch (25.5-cm) rope. To create the twist, use your palms to roll one end of the rope away from you while rolling the other toward you. Without letting the rope untwist, lift up both ends of the rope and it will twist automatically.

Place the dough twists on a large greased baking sheet, spacing them out, and cover it with a cloth. Let them rise again for 45 minutes.

Meanwhile, prepare the cinnamon-sugar coating. In a shallow bowl, stir together the sugar and cinnamon. Set aside.

In a large pot, heat the oil to 325°F (165°C) over medium heat. Carefully slide the dough twists, a few at a time, into the oil and fry on 1 side until they're deep golden brown, 60 to 90 seconds. Turn the dough over and continue to deep-fry them until they're deep golden brown, adjusting the heat so that they don't brown too quickly.

Remove the donuts from the oil and place them on a paper towel–lined plate to absorb any excess oil. Transfer them quickly to the cinnamon sugar and coat them well. Serve warm or at room temperature.

## (YAKSHIK, 약식)

# SWEET CHESTNUT STICKY RICE BARS

## MAKES 12 BARS

2 cups (400 g) sweet or glutinous short grain rice

10 dried jujubes

2 cups (480 ml) water

½ cup (113 g) dark brown sugar

2 tbsp (30 ml) soy sauce

1 tsp dark soy sauce (optional)

¼ tsp ground cinnamon

14 to 16 peeled fresh chestnuts, or 13 oz (370 g) canned, drained

2 tbsp (18 g) pine nuts or walnuts

3 tbsp (26 g) pumpkin seeds

1 tbsp (15 ml) sesame oil

Yakshik is a classic Korean sweet treat made with sweet glutinous short grain rice, chestnuts and dried jujubes. Mildly sweetened with dark brown sugar and a hint of cinnamon, it is known as a healthy snack typically served during the New Year or fall harvest holidays, but you don't need to wait for a special occasion. These bars freeze beautifully, so they are perfect as a quick breakfast on the go or afternoon snack when hunger hits. Instead of steaming these in the traditional way, which takes a long time, you can prepare this enchanting treat conveniently in a rice cooker or electric pressure cooker. Make sure you soak the rice the night before for at least six hours.

Rinse the sweet rice several times and place it in a large bowl. Pour in plenty of water and let the rice soak for at least 6 hours in the fridge.

Using a paring knife, slice the flesh off the dried jujubes to separate it from their seeds and set aside. Put the seeds in a small pot and pour in the water. Bring it to a boil and simmer for 5 minutes, or until the water becomes dark amber in color.

In a medium bowl, whisk together 1 cup (240 ml) of the jujube stock and the brown sugar, soy sauce, dark soy sauce (if using) and cinnamon. Whisk well until the sugar dissolves.

Drain the rice and place it in a rice cooker or electric pressure cooker. Add the sliced jujube flesh and the chestnuts. Pour in the brown sugar mixture and mix well. Cook at the normal setting on the rice cooker. If using an electric pressure cooker, use the rice setting with 12 minutes of cooking time, making sure to seal the vent. Let the steam release naturally.

When the cooking is done, add the pine nuts and pumpkin seeds. Drizzle in the sesame oil and gently toss everything well.

Line a 9-inch (23-cm) square pan with a piece of plastic wrap. Turn out the rice mixture into the prepared pan and press down with a spatula. Let it sit on a wire rack to cool. When fully cooled, remove the rice mixture from the pan and cut it into bars.

To freeze, wrap the bars tightly with a piece of plastic wrap, and then put them in a resealable plastic freezer bag. To thaw, let them sit at room temperature until fully thawed in their wrap, or remove the wrap and microwave on a plate for 2 minutes, or until soft.

**COOK'S TIP:** If you can't find dried jujubes or chestnuts, try ½ cup (80 g) of dried cranberries and/or raisins and walnuts.

## (COCONUT CHAPSSALTTOEK, 코코넛찹쌀떡)

# COCONUT RICE CAKE NUT BARS
## MAKES 8 BARS

Cooking oil spray

1½ cups (150 g) assorted nuts and seeds of your choice (walnuts, pecans, almonds, pistachios, sunflower seeds, pumpkin seeds, etc.), coarsely chopped

2 cups (316 g) sweet rice flour

1 cup (225 g) light brown sugar

½ tsp baking powder

¼ tsp salt

1¼ cups (300 ml) coconut milk

½ cup (about 72 g) dried fruit(s), such as raisins, dates, apricots or cranberries (chopped, if needed)

½ cup (43 g) sweetened coconut flakes

3 tbsp (55 g) sliced almonds

These oven-baked rice cake bars were created by Korean immigrants who settled in California, especially early arrivals to the Los Angeles area. Finding themselves far from their home country, their craving for traditional steamed rice cake needed to be adapted to an oven-baked method in their new Western-style kitchens. They didn't realize that they ended up creating healthy Korean granola bars. They are gluten-free, with no butter or oil! These bars are crispy on the outside, but they have a mochi-like chewy texture inside. Loaded with nuts, seeds and dried fruits, they are perfect as an on-the-go breakfast or as a quick energy bar for outdoor activities. I like to add coconut milk to the batter, which makes the bar richer in taste and subtly fragrant. Toast the nuts and seeds before you add them to the batter. It makes them even nuttier!

Preheat the oven to 375°F (190°C).

Spray an 8- to 9-inch (20.5- to 23-cm) square baking pan with cooking oil spray and line the bottom with parchment paper that extends beyond the opposite ends of the pan so that you can easily lift the cake out of the pan.

In a dry skillet, toast the nuts and seeds over medium heat until they are lightly golden, 2 to 3 minutes, stirring or shaking the skillet frequently so they get toasted evenly. Transfer them to a plate and set aside to cool.

In a bowl, whisk together the sweet rice flour, brown sugar, baking powder and salt. Add the coconut milk and whisk well. Add the toasted nuts and the dried fruit(s) to the mixing bowl and stir well with a spatula. Pour it into the prepared pan. Sprinkle the coconut flakes and sliced almonds on top.

Bake the mixture for 35 to 40 minutes, or until a toothpick inserted into the center comes out clean. Let it cool in the pan for 5 minutes, then remove it from the pan and let it cool completely on a wire rack. Cut it into 8 equal-size bars.

**COOK'S TIP:** These bars freeze beautifully. Wrap each bar with a piece of plastic wrap and place them in a resealable plastic freezer bag. Freeze them for up to 2 months. You can eat them right out of the freezer or let them thaw on the counter for 20 minutes.

## (TTALGI BINGSU, 딸기빙수)

# SHAVED MILKY ICE WITH STRAWBERRIES
## SERVES 4

3 cups (720 ml) whole milk

½ cup (120 ml) light or heavy cream

½ cup (100 g) granulated sugar, divided

1 lb (455 g) fresh strawberries, hulled and thinly sliced

¼ cup (60 ml) sweetened condensed milk

Blueberries, for garnish (optional)

Shaved ice is one of the most common sweet desserts you will find in Korea on hot summer days. Frozen milk is shaved into light snowflakes mimicking snow and adorned with sweetened red beans or fresh fruits. Here is one with strawberries, which is a favorite of mine. Mango, peach or blueberries are great choices, too. But what if you don't have an ice-shaving machine? No worries! You can make this recipe without a machine and it is so easy and good.

In a bowl, combine the milk, cream and 6 tablespoons (78 g) of the sugar. Whisk until the sugar dissolves. Pour the mixture in a gallon-size (3.8-L) resealable plastic bag. Place the bag on its side, lying flat, in the freezer and freeze for at least 3 hours.

Before serving the milky ice, in a bowl, combine the strawberry slices with the remaining 2 tablespoons (25 g) of sugar. Set it aside for 5 minutes to sweat a little.

Meanwhile, remove the bag from the freezer and let it sit at room temperature for 5 minutes to soften a little. Using a rolling pin, smack the bag to break up the milky ice. Turn the bag back and forth to the other side until you see the ice break down to small clusters.

Spoon the milky ice into individual serving bowls and top them with the strawberries. Drizzle the sweetened condensed milk over the strawberries and garnish with blueberries, if using. Serve immediately.

**COOK'S TIP:** When you freeze the milk mixture in the freezer, place the serving bowls in the freezer as well. The cold bowl will keep the shaved ice cold until the very last bite of your sweet treat.

## (GYEPI SAENGGANGCHA, 계피생강차)

2 oz (56 g) cinnamon sticks

10 dried jujubes

12 cups (2.8 L) water, divided

5 oz (140 g) fresh ginger, peeled and sliced

¼ to ½ cup (50 to 100 g) granulated sugar

½ cup (113 g) light brown sugar

Pine nuts, for garnish (optional)

# COLD REMEDY CINNAMON-GINGER TEA
## SERVES 10 TO 12 (6 CUPS [1.5 LITERS])

This "tea" will comfort you, body and soul. It is similar to the famous Korean sweet drink sujeonggwa. It's not really a tea because there are no tea leaves in the recipe. I call it my cold remedy tea, because with the body-warming cinnamon and ginger, it will help soothe cold symptoms when served hot. It is also great to serve chilled as a punch like sujeonggwa. If you want to maximize the fragrance and spiciness of the cinnamon and ginger, it is better to simmer them separately. However, you will still have a delightful beverage even if you simmer them together.

In a medium, lidded pot, combine the cinnamon sticks and dried jujubes with 6 cups (1.4 L) of the water. Cover it and bring it to a boil over high heat. Lower the heat to low and simmer for 30 minutes.

Meanwhile, in another medium, lidded pot, combine the ginger slices and the remaining 6 cups (1.4 L) of water. Bring it to a boil and simmer over low heat for 30 minutes.

Strain both liquids through a fine strainer into a third pot. Discard the cinnamon, ginger and jujubes. Add the sugars and heat it through to dissolve them completely. Adjust the sweetness according to your preference. Serve hot or chilled, garnished with pine nuts, if using.

**COOK'S TIP:** To convert this tea into an elegant Korean dessert punch (sujeonggwa), soak dried persimmon or dates in a little bit of this tea for 1 hour to moisten. Keep the tea chilled until ready to serve. When serving, pour the chilled tea over the softened fruits in a serving bowl or cup and garnish with pine nuts.

**(LEMON CHUNG, 레몬청)**

# KOREAN LEMON SYRUP DRINK
## MAKES ABOUT 3 PINTS (1.4 L)

2¼ lb (1 kg) lemons
Salt
Baking soda
2¼ lb (1 kg) sugar
Chilled carbonated water (for lemonade)
or hot water (for lemon tea)
Mint leaves, for garnish (optional)

Lemon chung is a lemon syrup made from whole lemons. It is a popular kitchen staple in Korea. You can use this syrup to make a cold drink or a hot citrus tea. You can also use it to make savory dishes, such as lemon chicken, or in a salad dressing. Make sure to pick out all the seeds from the lemon slices; otherwise they can make the syrup slightly bitter in taste. The ratio of lemon to sugar is usually 1:1—this helps prevent any mold so the syrup can last months in the fridge. It is important to clean the lemons very thoroughly at the outset to get rid of any pesticides remaining on the skin.

Rinse the lemons with water and rub the skin with the salt and baking soda. Then, rinse them with hot water. The lemon skin should feel soft and smooth. Wipe the lemons with a dry, clean kitchen towel.

Slice the lemons into ¼-inch (6-mm)-thick slices. Discard the ends of the lemons, and pick out all the seeds from the lemon slices.

In a large, nonmetal bowl, mix the lemon slices with the sugar. Transfer the sugared lemon slices to a sterilized airtight 2-quart (1.9-L) glass jar. Seal the jar with a lid and let it sit at room temperature for 1 to 2 days, shaking the jar a couple of times every once in a while, until the sugar dissolves completely. Store it in the fridge for 3 days before you use the syrup.

To serve as cold lemonade, put a few slices of lemon and its juice in a glass and pour in chilled carbonated water. Adjust the amount of lemon slices and its juice in your drink according to your taste. Garnish with mint leaves, if using.

To serve as hot citrus tea, use hot water instead. Adding a couple of thin slices of fresh ginger will turn your hot lemon tea into a comforting lemon-ginger tea—perfect for cold weather.

# KOREAN PANTRY

## ANCHOVY SAUCE (MYULCHI ACKJEOT, 멸치액젓)

Anchovy sauce is basically an extract from fermented anchovies. It is used widely to make various types of kimchi. It also adds a pungent flavor in Korean soups and stews. Store the sauce in a dark place at room temperature.

## BLACK BEAN PASTE (CHUNJANG, 짜장)

Chunjang sauce is a type of black bean sauce. This sauce is mainly for making the famous noodle dish that bears its name (jjajangmyun) or a similarly-flavored rice dish (jjanjagbap). It has a bitter edge to it, so I recommend frying it in oil with a little bit of sugar before adding it to a recipe. You can also buy a preroasted version of this sauce that doesn't require that step. Keep the sauce in the fridge once opened.

## DRIED ANCHOVIES (MYULCHI, 마른멸치)

Dried anchovies come in different sizes. The large anchovies are generally for making soup stock. The medium and small sizes are more for stir-fried dishes. Store dried anchovies in the freezer to prevent any mold.

## DRIED JUJUBE (DAECHU, 대추)

High in nutrition, dried jujubes are used in many Korean drinks as a health supplement. They are also used in many savory dishes to add an aroma and sweetness. Keep the jujube in an airtight bag and store it in the freezer.

## DRIED SEA KELP (DASHIMA, 다시마)

Dried sea kelp is widely used with dried anchovies to make the stock base for soups and stews. I recommend purchasing a package of whole sea kelp and cutting it yourself to the size you need. Keep your dried sea kelp in an airtight container and store it in a dry, dark, cool environment.

## DRIED SEAWEED (MIYUK, 미역)

This feather-light ribbon seaweed is mainly for soups and salads. You will need to soak it in water to rehydrate the seaweed before using it in recipes. After soaking for just ten minutes, it will expand to more than quadruple in volume, so use less than you think you'll need. Store it in a dark, dry place.

## DRIED SEAWEED SHEETS (GIM, 김)

These dried seaweed sheets are unseasoned and unroasted, so they are ready to use in recipes. Preseasoned and roasted seaweeds are available in most grocery stores, but roasting your seaweed at home is much healthier and incredibly easy. Look for seaweed sheets that are black with a slight green tint. Avoid any seaweed that has a red tint. Store the seaweed in the freezer since it can go rancid at room temperature.

*Left—from top left to bottom right: salted shrimp, Korean pastes ( fermented soybean paste, chili paste, seasoned soybean paste), citron tea, plum extract, herb packet, chili flakes, dried anchovies, sweet potato noodles, wheat noodles (different thicknesses)*

## KOREAN CHILI FLAKES (GOCHUGARU, 고추가루)

Korean chili flakes, also known as Korean chili powder or red pepper powder, come in two types: coarse or fine. Fine chili powder is used to make gochujang (chili paste), whereas coarse chili flakes are mostly used in cooking. Korean chili flakes cannot be replaced by South American-style "chili powder" or other chili powder from a different cuisine. Korean chili flakes come from Korea's red finger-long chiles. They are not overly hot compared to the other chiles. I would recommend getting Korean-origin chili flakes, if possible. They will be twice the price of other varieties, but well worth it for the outcome. Always keep chili flakes in the freezer to prevent mold.

## KOREAN CHILI PASTE (GOCHUJANG, 고추장)

You can't have enough Korean chili paste if you love Korean food. One of the most beloved Korean condiments of all, it is spicy and addictive. You can find mild chili paste for those who are wary of spiciness. Gochujang is a very fine chili powder made with rice or barley (and sometimes wheat), fermented soybean powder, salt and a little bit of malt. Once opened, store it in the fridge.

## KOREAN FERMENTED SOYBEAN PASTE (DOENJANG, 된장)

Korean soybean paste, made of fermented soybeans, is a rich source of good bacteria, *Bacillus subtilis*. The best way to absorb these good bacteria into your body is to eat doenjang raw as a topping sauce because these bacteria don't hold up very well in the heat. Doenjang paste is quite strong in flavor and odor. Although it features prominently in soups and stews, it also seasons some meat and vegetable dishes. Keep the sauce in the fridge once opened.

## KOREAN HERB PACKET

This packet is mainly for making Korean chicken and ginseng soup (samgyetang). Many exotic Korean or Asian medical supplemental herbs are included. All the ingredients you need to make the soup are in the packet, so it makes cooking this dish surprisingly convenient. There are many different varieties you can choose from, but I would avoid the one with sweet rice included (you can always add it on your own). Although many of the herb packets might not contain dried ginseng, it still makes the soup very fragrant and delicious.

## KOREAN MUSTARD (YEONGYEOJA, 연겨자)

This is Korean prepared mustard. Its very sharp flavor is reminiscent of wasabi and adds a sinus-clearing piquancy to many Korean dishes. It is sold in tubes and needs to be kept in the fridge.

## KOREAN OLIGO SYRUP (OLIGO-DANG, 올리고당)

Several different varieties of sweet syrups are used in Korean cooking: corn syrup, rice syrup and oligo syrup. Corn syrup is well known in the United States, but rice syrup and oligo syrup are more widely used in Korea. Rice syrup is from rice, of course. Oligo syrup is an oligosaccharide that is extracted from fruits and vegetables. It is similar to fructose but is a more simple sugar, and is perhaps a healthier alternative to corn syrup since it is less sweet and has more fiber than ordinary sugar. Outside of Korea, you probably need to go to your local Korean grocer to find oligo sugar. Keep the syrup in a dark place at room temperature.

## KOREAN PEARS (BAE, 배)

Korean pears are large—even larger than most Asian pears. They are very round and have golden brown skin. The flesh is very crisp, like an apple's, but even juicier and very sweet. Korean pears are wonderful to eat as a snack. One pear can serve two to four people. They also serve as an important ingredient to marinate and flavor meat in Korean cooking. You can find them in Korean or Asian stores during fall and winter. They can last in the refrigerator up to one month if wrapped in paper.

## KOREAN PLUM EXTRACT (MAESHIL-CHEONG, 매실청)

This natural, sweet syrup is made from marinated Korean green plums and sugar. It is generally used in Korean dishes that require a little sweetness. You can dilute the syrup with cold water and drink it as a beverage. You can omit the plum extract from most recipes in this cookbook, but if you enjoy cooking Korean food often, it is great to have one bottle in your kitchen. Once opened, store it in the fridge.

## KOREAN SALTED SHRIMP (SAEWOO-JEOT, 새우젓)

These tiny shrimps are salted and fermented. They are mostly used to make kimchi. However, you can add a tiny amount of salted shrimp to your soups and stews, and even to your side dishes to deepen the flavor. Always keep the salted shrimp in the fridge.

## KOREAN SEASONED SOYBEAN PASTE (SSAMJANG, 쌈장)

This is a type of dipping sauce that is a mixture of soybean paste, chili paste, onion, garlic and other spices. This sauce is used to top grilled meat or vegetable wraps, or simply to use as a dip for vegetable sticks. Once opened, store it in the fridge.

## KOREAN SOY SAUCE FOR SOUP (GUK-GANJANG, 국간장)

Korean soy sauce for soup is a traditional variety of Korean soy sauce unique to Korean cooking. It is also often called josun ganjang, with josun referring to the historical name for Korea. It is saltier and more translucent than regular soy sauce. It adds a pungency to certain Korean dishes without altering the natural flavor of the dish itself. As the name says, the sauce is widely used to season soups, stews and various vegetable side dishes. Refrigerate it after opening.

## RICE CAKES (TTEOKPPOKI TTEOK, 떡볶이 떡)

There are two types of rice cakes: Flat, round rice cakes are for soups, and the rice cake sticks are used in stir-fries. Look for rice cakes that are made with 100 percent rice if you want to avoid gluten, because some rice cakes contain wheat. Fresh rice cakes are also available at many Korean stores, but they need to be consumed the same day they are made. Most packaged rice cakes are found in the refrigerated section and you will need to soak them in water before using them in recipes, to achieve their ideal smooth texture.

## SWEET POTATO NOODLES (DANGMYUN, 당면)

Dangmyun refers to dried noodles made of sweet potato starch. They have a gray tint when dried, but become translucent when cooked in water. The noodles themselves do not have any particular taste, so they are like a blank canvas to which you can add the artistry of your flavor. Their chewiness makes them very satisfying to eat. The most famous dish made with dangmyun noodles is japchae. After boiling the noodles in water until soft, you will need to rinse them in cold water to maintain their trademark chewiness, unless you intend to put them in stews or other braised dishes.

## SWEET RICE FLOUR (CHAPSSALGARU, 찹쌀가루)

Sweet rice (also known as glutinous rice, even though it does not contain any gluten) is what makes this rice flour "sweet." Korean sweet rice flour comes from short-grain glutinous rice and is widely used in both savory and sweet dishes. Keep sweet rice flour in an airtight container or bag and store it in a dark, dry place.

## KOREAN TUNA SAUCE (CHAMCHI-ACK, 참치액)

This is an extract from fermented tuna fish. It has a unique smoky flavor that brings a depth to many soups and stews. Store the sauce in a dark place at room temperature.

## WILD SESAME OIL (DELGIRUM, 들기름)

Wild sesame oil (aka perilla oil) comes from perilla plant seeds. Perilla leaves are commonly eaten in Korea. Although perilla leaves themselves have a strong fragrance, the oil extracted from perilla seeds is milder than sesame oil. Store it in a dark place at room temperature.

*Right—from top left to bottom right: tuna sauce, wild sesame oil, anchovy sauce, Korean pears, oligo syrup, Korean mustard, dried seaweed sheets and dried seaweed, sweet glutenous short grain rice, rice cakes*

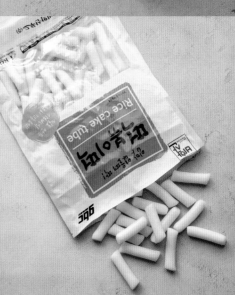

# ACKNOWLEDGMENTS

Writing this book brought me great joy and fulfillment, and I would like to share my appreciation for my loved ones.

Thanks to my mother in Korea for the example and the lessons she taught me. Her unconditional love and devotion made me who I am now.

Thanks to my father, who passed away twelve years ago, for the enthusiasm and creativity he shared with me during his life. I wish I could share this book with him. He would have been my #1 fan. I miss you, Dad.

Thanks to my husband, Ben, for his support and encouragement. His honest review of my dishes helped me create better recipes each time. I appreciate his patience in proofreading all the recipes in this book.

Thanks to my daughter, Lauren, for coming up with the chapter titles in this book. Her love of Korean food motivated me to start the entire journey of Korean cooking from the beginning. I hope she will cherish this book and carry on our Korean heritage in the family.

Thanks to my son, Preston, for cheering me up throughout the process of creating this book. He is not the strongest advocate for the spicy and sometimes fermented flavor of Korean food yet, but I believe he will be eventually.

Lastly, I'd like to give thanks to Rebecca, an associate editor at Page Street Publishing Company, for giving me the opportunity to share my creations and guiding me throughout the process.

# ABOUT THE AUTHOR

Hyegyoung (aka Holly) was born and raised in South Korea and later moved to the United States to earn a degree in fashion design. She worked in the fashion industry in both Seoul and Boston.

After she started a family, her children grew up loving Korean food. Her desire to pass on her home recipes and stories to her children inspired her to document her Korean recipes and experiences in an online cooking blog. She shared many of her personal recipes and stories in her blog, Beyond Kimchee. Although the blog was originally intended as a gift for her children, through it Hyegyoung connected with countless people around the world. Her blog is one of the top English-language Korean cooking blogs.

As a cook, Hyegyoung is self-taught, but of course owes a debt of gratitude to her mother and the generations before her. Hyegyoung's recipes have been featured in many publications, including *Go Gluten-Free Magazine* and *Food and Travel* magazine, Singapore. She has written several food columns for The *Korean Daily* newspaper and Dramafever.com.

Hyegyoung lives in northern Virginia with her husband, two children and their most adorable labradoodle named Nabi.

# INDEX